SpringerBriefs in Criminology

SpringerBriefs in Policing

Series Editor
M. R. Haberfeld, John Jay College of Criminal Justice
City University of New York
New York, NY, USA

SpringerBriefs in Criminology present concise summaries of cutting edge research across the fields of Criminology and Criminal Justice. It publishes small but impactful volumes of between 50-125 pages, with a clearly defined focus. The series covers a broad range of Criminology research from experimental design and methods, to brief reports and regional studies, to policy-related applications.

The scope of the series spans the whole field of Criminology and Criminal Justice, with an aim to be on the leading edge and continue to advance research. The series will be international and cross-disciplinary, including a broad array of topics, including juvenile delinquency, policing, crime prevention, terrorism research, crime and place, quantitative methods, experimental research in criminology, research design and analysis, forensic science, crime prevention, victimology, criminal justice systems, psychology of law, and explanations for criminal behavior.

SpringerBriefs in Criminology will be of interest to a broad range of researchers and practitioners working in Criminology and Criminal Justice Research and in related academic fields such as Sociology, Psychology, Public Health, Economics and Political Science.

SpringerBriefs in Policing presents concise summaries of cutting edge research in Police Science, across the fields of Criminology, Criminal Justice, Psychology, Forensic Science, and Corrections with implications for the study of police and police work. It publishes small but impactful volumes of between 50-125 pages, with a clearly defined focus. The series covers a broad range of Policing research: from experimental design and methods, to brief reports and regional case studies, to policy-related applications. The scope of the series spans the subfield of Policing, with an aim to be on the leading edge and continue to advance research. The series is international and cross-disciplinary, including a broad array of topics. The main goal of the series is to present innovations in Policing, in order to further the field as a research and evidence-based profession rather than a vocational occupation. It will showcase how Policing confronts problems and challenges that transcend cultures and borders and can be addressed from a global rather than local perspective. SpringerBriefs in Policing is aimed at a broad range of researchers and practitioners working in Criminology and Criminal Justice Research and in related academic fields such as Public Policy, Sociology, Psychology, Public Health, Economics, Policy Analysis, Terrorism and Political Science.

Rainer Kroll

Internal Investigations for Law Enforcement

Rainer Kroll
Western Connecticut State University
Danbury, CT, USA

ISSN 2192-8533　　　　　　ISSN 2192-8541　(electronic)
SpringerBriefs in Criminology
ISSN 2194-6213　　　　　　ISSN 2194-6221　(electronic)
SpringerBriefs in Policing
ISBN 978-3-031-21526-1　　ISBN 978-3-031-21527-8　(eBook)
https://doi.org/10.1007/978-3-031-21527-8

© The Author(s), under exclusive license to Springer Nature Switzerland AG 2023
This work is subject to copyright. All rights are solely and exclusively licensed by the Publisher, whether the whole or part of the material is concerned, specifically the rights of translation, reprinting, reuse of illustrations, recitation, broadcasting, reproduction on microfilms or in any other physical way, and transmission or information storage and retrieval, electronic adaptation, computer software, or by similar or dissimilar methodology now known or hereafter developed.
The use of general descriptive names, registered names, trademarks, service marks, etc. in this publication does not imply, even in the absence of a specific statement, that such names are exempt from the relevant protective laws and regulations and therefore free for general use.
The publisher, the authors, and the editors are safe to assume that the advice and information in this book are believed to be true and accurate at the date of publication. Neither the publisher nor the authors or the editors give a warranty, expressed or implied, with respect to the material contained herein or for any errors or omissions that may have been made. The publisher remains neutral with regard to jurisdictional claims in published maps and institutional affiliations.

This Springer imprint is published by the registered company Springer Nature Switzerland AG
The registered company address is: Gewerbestrasse 11, 6330 Cham, Switzerland

To Dr. Maria Haberfeld, John Jay College of Criminal Justice, and Dr. Mitch Librett, Bridgewater University, whose guidance and patience made this work possible.

Contents

Introduction 1
Reference 2

Internal Investigations Context 3
References 6

Politics Behind Internal Investigations 7
References 8

Supervisor's Role in Internal Investigations 11
Problems with Internal Investigations 11
Supervisory Challenges in Conducting Internal Investigations 12
Good and Bad Investigations 14
References 15

Investigative Perspective; Organizational, Cultural Behavior 17
Underlying Theory of Police Misconduct/Corruption 18
References 20

A Continuum of Incident Classifications 21
Types of Allegations 22
Initial Investigations 23
Case Assessment and Classification 24
Typical Investigations and Suggested Investigative Steps-Introduction 25
Common Investigative Steps 25
Proactive Measures 29
Administering an Integrity Test 29
References 30

Interviewing the Subject 33
References 34

Occupational Crimes Specific to the Role of Police Officers-Introduction 35
Missing Property Allegations 35
Fraud 38
Association with Criminals 38
Planting/Padding Evidence (Flaking) Allegations 39
Narcotics Allegations 39
Drug Use Allegations 41
Drug Screening Failure 42
Police Officer-Involved DWI Arrests 43
Domestic Incidents Involving Police Officers 44
Force Incidents 46
False Statements/Perjury 48
Quota Allegation 49
Processing an Arrested Officer 50
Changing an Officer's Duty Status 51
Monitoring Court Proceedings 52
Case Closing Reports 52
Investigative Dispositions 55
Completing Investigations 55
References 56

Lessons Learned 57
Proper Mindset 57
Case Investigations 58
Interviews 58
Evidence 59
Reliance on Others 59
Timelines 60
Dealing with Subjects 60
Noncompliant Complainants 61
Consequences of an Internal Investigation 61
Concluding Remarks 62
Types of Cases Chart 62
References 63

Additional Resources 65

Index 67

Introduction

This brief is designed to inform the police literature by providing organized guidelines and recommendations on how to conduct police internal investigations. If the agency has a comprehensive training program on how to conduct these investigations, along with the necessary resources to succeed, then the investigator is truly prepared. In that event, I congratulate the investigator in their efforts. Too often though, training in conducting these investigations is incomplete, offered piecemeal, provided as much by word of mouth as organized training, which leaves gaps in investigative knowledge. It would be unrealistic to provide a comprehensive, all-inclusive guide to cover every possible scenario. That is primarily due to the vastly diverse composition and size of the agencies responsible for maintaining public safety in America today. The resources and subcultural structures of over 18,000 independent police departments providing police services is simply too diverse and vastly independent to suggest any one model of internal investigations (Walker & Katz, 2017).

In this brief, I provide investigative techniques, to be applied generally. This makes a comprehensive guidebook unnecessary. This brief helps fill the gaps through lived experience and extensive knowledge.

Whether a seasoned internal investigator, or newly assigned to this type of work, this brief can assist in the investigator's duties. The seasoned investigator can benefit from what may be differing perspectives, which can be used to supplement their efforts. The novice investigator can benefit by following the investigative plans provided in the brief. They are sound guidelines, able to withstand external scrutiny. Coupled with agency policies and guidelines, the brief supplements a solid, professional investigation.

Reference

Walker, S., & Katz, C. (2017). *Police in America: An introduction* (9th ed.). McGraw Hill Publishing.

Internal Investigations Context

In general, investigations in law enforcement are a retrospective inquiry into incidents. Just like crime scene reconstructions, investigators go about determining the facts of an event. It is this pursuit of the factual circumstances of this event that drives modern investigative practice. Internal investigations are no different. The investigator is searching for the truth, but they are dealing with law enforcement employees. As such, these investigations are extremely important and sensitive, both for the agency and the individual employee. The investigator is obligated to conduct a professional, impartial inquiry to determine what occurred.

Internal investigations in law enforcement are a necessary part of the police function and are instrumental to the organization. Complete and accurate investigation of allegations against police officers and civilian employee are important for the employees, the community, and the political climate the agency operates in. In fact, internal investigations, and how they are handled, attest to the very legitimacy of the police organization. Communities that do not perceive that their police agencies are providing procedural justice are communities that cannot achieve the position of "co-producers of crime control" (USDOJ, 1989). Hence, effective, and impartial internal investigations are important and will enhance the relationship between any given police department and the community it serves. These very important investigations need to be completed thoroughly and properly.

Police misconduct and criminality have taken on a new significance in light of local events with national implications. Although incidents of police corruption and misconduct have occurred since the advent of policing, the prevalence of fatalities occurring during seemingly routine police interactions have become part of the national consciousness. They have become the most extreme instances of police, citizen interactions. The civilian responses to these incidents are, for the most part, violent, highlighting the frustrations and lack of trust and communication between the police and the public they are sworn to protect. In fact, the very foundation of policing is shaken to its core with notorious incidents occurring while in police custody. It is important to note here, police custody is taken to mean an interaction with the police, where the civilian is not necessarily free to leave (Walker & Katz, 2017).

While the foregoing example is offered as a reminder of the hazards of policing, it is in no way, an indictment of any officer's actions. That is for the local district attorney to decide. What it does highlight, is the extremely important nature of internal investigations. It is imperative to capture the facts, and create a permanent record of the event, as soon as possible after the incident.

It is important to note that there is no single, best way to conduct investigations. There are many ways to collect information to create the story of what occurred. With experience, the investigator will find, however, that certain types of investigations are unique and require specific techniques to create this record. An example would be an allegation of theft of prisoner property, one of the most frequent allegations made against police officers Not all agencies have similar procedures to account for this type of property allegation. Another example would be an allegation of credit card fraud. Both of these allegations require a different investigative path to contribute to a final conclusion, which is the documentation of what occurred (Gehl, 2017).

The investigator may have the benefit of access to the vast realm of experience in conducting these investigations. Tenured investigators have accumulated a vast amount of institutional knowledge in conducting investigations, which can be of great benefit to those willing to listen. Others may not have this benefit and find themselves in a position where they are operating alone. This is partly due to the sensitive and confidential nature of these investigations, which creates difficulties in accessing an institutional knowledge base. It is for those investigators that are working without the benefit of others that this brief is written. It intends to fill, partially, this lack of available information. It is also written for the seasoned investigator, who may benefit from a different investigative perspective, or a refresher.

In writing this brief, the author was able to benefit from a multi-faceted career, developing a well-rounded perspective from experiences in street-level policing to administrative and managerial assignments. Internal investigations comprised approximately 7 years of a 35 year career, 23 of which were in middle management. During this tenure, the author learned how to investigate, manage a team, and learned many of the unique steps required in these investigations. A typical caseload of 20–30 cases was not uncommon.

It would be impossible, within the scope of this brief, to cover all the steps in an internal investigation. It would be simplest to provide a list of investigative steps for different allegations, but that tends to limit investigations to the steps and miss the additional investigative steps unique to each incident that are uncovered during the case work. Further, there is the debate regarding whether any given police agency is capable of effectively and impartially investigating members of their own agencies. This issue lies beyond the scope of this document.

The push for outside investigation to avoid the appearance of conflicts of interest is largely governed by a few factors. First, the size of the agency has a large impact on the makeup of internal investigations. Large police departments have the capacity to establish stand-alone units staffed by investigators that are specially trained and assigned to this task. In this case, the socio-spatial distance between internal investigators and the mainstream of the agency does, in my opinion, reduce the possibility of bias; in a very small agency, recusal and referral to an outside authority may be an option. It is my belief that proper training and selection of the investigator(s) can eliminate the need for it. The other factors are regional differences in social attitudes and assumptions can impact upon the decision to either recuse in favor of outside oversight or retain the process as a routine function of departmental protocols. For example, in Massachusetts, the State Police are by state law the lead investigators in all homicides outside of the City of Boston. They provide units attached to the offices of the various district attorneys, and work directly under the authority of the district attorney. The decision to assign these state-level investigators to investigate allegations of police misconduct is made by the district attorney and in the vast majority of instances this option is exercised. This is necessitated in states such as Massachusetts where local police hold no authority as police officers beyond the bounds of their geographical area of employment. In New York and most other states-police officers hold at least some authority to enforce criminal law statewide. State police in New York play a relatively insignificant role in local law enforcement; the general public does not perceive them as an oversight agency, and indeed have no official mandate to assume this role. If done properly, any police agency is capable of performing unbiased and effective investigations of misconduct (UNODC, 2011).

What this brief will do is introduce investigative techniques for specific types of allegations and offer insight into developing the proper investigative mindset required to engage in what is traditionally identified as toxic, distasteful work. This work is toxic because it is contrary to the very essence of police subculture. Police officers belong to a group that is socially excluded because of the nature of their work and gravitate towards each other within this socially isolated group. This creates the Us versus Them and the Thin Blue Line mentality. It is the police officers that are protecting society from chaos and anarchy and if the investigator are not part of the group, the investigator is considered an outsider. Internal investigators are a group outside of the traditional police subculture and are regarded with contempt, even hatred, and mistrust. The internal investigator is the embodiment of everything that is contrary to the police subculture (Caldero et al., 2018).

This brief is useful for several reasons. It provides various investigative steps required for different allegations. It also serves as a refresher for an allegation that may not be that common, or as a way to consider alternate investigative steps. Remember, there are no absolutes in these investigations, but they can provide guidelines to follow, or at the very least, consider.

This brief can also assist in developing an internal investigative policy in an agency. There is enough information to assist those assigned to investigate an allegation against a law enforcement employee. The lists are relevant and go a long way towards conducting a complete, professional investigation, because they can serve as a reference guide for an investigative plan. These investigations are unique and relatively infrequent in smaller departments. The ultimate purpose is to conduct a complete and thorough investigation. This is not without some difficulty though, due to the complexity of certain complaints.

There are numerous social expectations to these investigations, within the police agency and the communities they serve. This is due to a heightened level of social scrutiny of the police. Besides the internal agency requirements to conduct a comprehensive and thorough investigation, the community expects a similar effort from the investigator. There is a certain mistrust of agencies policing themselves, and not without cause. Anytime there is a scandal, and the Federal Government needs to step in with oversight, this whittles away at the agency's reputation. The Department of Justice is mandated to investigate civil rights violations, and this creates a dilemma for the police agency being investigated. To minimize this, internal investigations need to be thorough, conducted with the highest levels of integrity, openness, and honesty. These records can be reviewed by oversight committees, staffed with attorneys and experts within their fields. Passing their review with minor suggestions reflects personal choices in investigative styles, not the integrity of the investigation.

References

Caldero, M. A., Dailer, J. D., & Withrow, B. L. (2018). *Police ethics: The corruption of noble cause*. Routledge.

Gehl, R. (2017). *Introduction to criminal investigation: Processes, practices and thinking*. BCcampus.

United Nations Office on Drugs and Crime. (2011). *Handbook on police accountability, oversight and integrity*. United Nations Publication.

U.S. Department of Justice, Office of Justice Programs. (1989). *Perfect partners: Co-production and crime prevention*. https://www.ojp.gov/pdffiles1/Digitization/140663NCJRS.pdf

Walker, S., & Katz, C. (2017). *Police in America: An introduction* (9th ed.). McGraw Hill Publishing.

Politics Behind Internal Investigations

Policing in general and internal investigations in particular are extremely political. It is common knowledge that the police and local government have a tenuous relationship. As long as everything is going well, meaning there is no incident with the police garnering negative media attention, the police agency operates within the local government mandate. Within the police agency, incidents that require an internal investigation can be thought of similarly. As long as police operations continue unencumbered by incidents of corruption or misconduct, the agency maintains an equilibrium within the local government environment (USDOJ, 2000). It is when an incident occurs that upsets this equilibrium that police agencies must respond to restore the status quo. Notorious incidents are an embarrassment to the police agency and the local government. It suggests a certain incompetency, which in turn creates a crisis of management. Police agencies must constantly root out corruption and maintain standards of the highest integrity. It is this duality that creates a mandate for supervisors to be constantly vigilant, exercising extreme competence in managing these investigations.

Another important factor to consider is the inherent conflict between external and internal oversight of the police agency. Both have differing requirements for qualification and employment. This results in differing ideologies and operating paradigms (U.S. Commission on Civil Rights, 2000).

External oversight agencies begin with a distinct disadvantage in investigations. If not recruited with a law enforcement background, they conduct investigations without the benefit of lived experience in talking to people, reviewing evidence, for example, and all of the other investigative techniques officers learn in their careers. These external agencies, by their very nature, are protected from allegations of subversion and bias in their investigations (Bobb, n.d.). Internal oversight benefits from the advantage of this lived experience. As long as the investigators are carefully vetted for integrity before assignment, there tend to be minimal issues with their investigative work. This can be carefully controlled through quality assurance and audits.

Internal audits should be conducted through the investigative chain of command and an independent, internal audit. This tiered review process makes the evaluation more objective and impersonal, removing the potential for professional bias. Reviewing personnel should be trained in this process. This ensures a standardized format for conducting the review. The result is an audit where there will be little to challenge other than preferences of investigative steps.

A final consideration pertains to the personnel assigned to conduct investigations, whichever capacity they operate in. They need to be carefully vetted before assignment. They should have a predominantly positive service record and pass an interview process. They should be, whenever possible, be of a supervisory rank. Supervisors have a more developed perspective, based on their longevity within the agency, and are able to interview subordinates with greater ease, due to the superior/subordinate relationship. Police officers and detectives, on the other hand, need to undergo the same rigorous vetting process. If accepted, they can staff positions at an intake center, conduct undercover operations, and handle a normal investigative caseload. Their choices in choosing this line of work are numerous but make them vulnerable to chastisement and abuse by peers and supervisors alike (USDOJ, 2011).

A final thought concerns a candidate's personal perspectives regarding these types of investigations, which is based on their personal mindset. This mindset reflects the sum total of past experiences and colors a person's outlook. The interview should explore this dynamic and determine whether the applicant is able to conduct a fair, impartial, and objective investigation (Cuncic, 2022).

These personnel are taking on a task that is the antithesis of police culture. It is incumbent upon the supervisors to protect the team from the inevitable ostracism that will occur. This pervades police culture and will be found throughout a career within the unit. It can be handled easily with a good working relationship with other members of the agency and proper supervision of the team. It is, however, an extra supervisory burden not necessarily anticipated.

One final note in this section is the imperative that internal investigations and the staff be a separate entity from the remainder of the agency. If this is not possible due to the makeup of the agency, the next best thing is to ensure absolute confidentiality of all internal activities. Remember, these investigations can ruin careers, whether founded or not. That is why the only connection with the agency should be at the top echelons of the bureaucracy. The agency head needs to be kept informed, but beyond that, information should only be shared on a need-to-know basis. Even that should be carefully considered by the unit head, or their designee.

References

Bobb, M. (n.d.). *Internal and external police oversight in the United States.* https://www.prearesourcecenter.org/sites/default/files/library/internalandexternalpoliceoversightintheunitedstates.pdf

Cuncic, A. (2022, February 18). *The psychology behind police brutality.* Verywell Mind. https://www.verywellmind.com/the-psychology-behind-police-brutality-5077410

References

U.S. Department of Justice, Office of Justice Programs. (2000). *The measurement of police integrity*. https://www.ojp.gov/pdffiles1/nij/181465.pdf

U.S. Department of Justice, Office of Justice Programs. (2011). *Police discipline: A case for change*. https://www.ojp.gov/pdffiles1/nij/234052.pdf

United States Commission on Civil Rights. (2000) *Revisiting Who is guarding the guardians? A report on police practices and civil rights in America.* https://www.ojp.gov/pdffiles1/bja/249021.pdf

Supervisor's Role in Internal Investigations

The investigating supervisor's role in internal investigations is no different than any criminal investigation involving civilians. The only difference is that the subject is a fellow member of the service, which adds a certain complexity to the investigation. This complexity involves maintaining an objective outlook when steering the investigation. The supervisor must remain dispassionate, imparting this attitude on the case investigator. The investigation must consist of collecting the relevant facts as efficiently, and as objectively as possible. It is this investigative paradigm that will support all involved in several ways (USDOJ, 2003).

Being able to say that the investigation was conducted objectively, with due diligence, goes a long way of legitimizing the investigators and supervisors and the agency. Internal investigators are under considerable scrutiny to begin with, constantly protecting themselves from allegations of subjectivity and favoritism. They operate under the cloud of suspicion that they are advocates for the agency, protecting everyone from embarrassment. If the supervisors maintain the constant professionalism that these subject officers deserve, they protect themselves and the agency from these allegations.

Problems with Internal Investigations

There are numerous problems with conducting internal investigations. How well these are managed is an indicator of the quality of the investigation. These problems consist of personal and organizational qualities that investigators and their supervisors should be made aware of.

The first relevant issue is the quality of the investigation. High caliber investigations are the result of knowledge, training, experience, and attitude. Where these qualities are lacking, the quality suffers. The consequence can be dire for careers, if conducted poorly. Compounding this issue is the fact that the subject is a fellow agency employee. It is the investigator's role to make sure the investigation is fair, impartial, and completed in a timely manner. It is the supervisor's task to monitor the assigned investigator's progress and ensure that this occurs.

A second relevant issue concerns the organization. The overall climate must be conducive to a climate free of corruption and misconduct. This needs to be framed within the organizational mandate, otherwise there is the potential for problems. Maintaining the highest standards of integrity and professionalism goes a long way towards organizational legitimacy. Deviating from this mandate, leaves the organization open to incidents that reflect poorly on everyone within the organization. Integrity, human dignity, justice, professionalism, and leadership are the significant values the agency must embrace to have the legitimacy required to perform their mission (IACP, 2008).

Supervisory Challenges in Conducting Internal Investigations

There are about 18,000 police agencies within the United States that respond to citizen complaints and are expected to root out and suppress behaviors that have been criminalized within the geographical areas where they operate. There are a number of variables that impact on the structure, mandate, and size of the unit within each department responsible for identifying, monitoring, and assigning responsibility for misconduct (UNODC, 2011).

First, the size of the agency will control the nature of the internal affairs process. It is impossible for a small-town police department (10–50 officers) to maintain a full-time unit composed of experienced investigators that receive specialized training in "policing the police." These agencies typically do not receive a large number of complaints and will either assign general-duty detectives to investigate them or ask a county-level or state police agency to take the lead. The findings are forwarded and assessed by the agency head, who then will implement sanctions if warranted.

Second, public expectations can have a great impact on the way complaints are investigated, and by whom. For example, the states of Connecticut and Massachusetts have eliminated most county-level law enforcement. In Massachusetts, state law mandates that the Massachusetts State Police is the designated agency taking the lead when serving police officers are accused of criminal acts or serious misconduct. There is a strong public belief that members of the same agency cannot maintain an objective perspective if put in the position where they must conduct a possibly career-ending investigation involving another officer who the designated investigator has known personally (and perhaps socially) for years. The Office of District Attorneys in Massachusetts is enormously powerful and directs the activities of a unit of State Police assigned to each D.A.'s direct control. Contrast this with the State of New York, where the New York State Police has no mandate nor legal standing to assume this role. Occasionally either a county-level or specialized state police unit might be asked for technical assistance, typically with motor vehicle accident reconstruction. Large agencies, with thousands of officers, have increasingly come under pressure to allow specially constructed outside oversight agencies to conduct independent (and sometimes simultaneous) investigations arising from citizen complaints. An example of this would be the Citizens Complaint Review Board in the City of New York. At the macro level, following the upheaval within policing arising from the events in Ferguson, Missouri, and the death of George Floyd, big city police agencies have come under tremendous pressure to allow outside oversight processes to have the final say in sanctioning individual police officers, even to the extent of acquiring the power to override to decision of police Chiefs or Commissioners. Hence, it would be fair to say that the actions of individual police officers, criminal or not, will be increasingly subject to scrutiny by investigators and agencies outside of the wider police culture (Zacarese, 2016).

Internal investigations most often arise from relatively minor complaints such as discourtesy, becoming unfit for duty (most often referring to officers that become intoxicated while off duty and engaging in offensive but not criminal behavior), minor acts of defiance to a supervisor, involvement in an at-fault motor vehicle accident, clerical errors or laziness, etc. These acts of misconduct are typically sanctioned by the forfeiture of several days accumulated leave time and are rarely the source of public opprobrium. Structural differences in the internal review process have little impact on sanctioning minor acts of occupational deviance.

Use of force by police officers has become increasingly controversial. The YouTube world of almost universal video surveillance has, on the micro-level challenged internal investigators to become experts in both electronic surveillance and also acquire the ability to interpret video clips that can be jumbled, out of context, or deceptive. Therefore, the structure and/or size and mandate of an internal affairs process can impact tremendously upon police officers' careers and/or personal freedom. Moreover, with the elimination of qualified immunity for police officers, internal investigators must be prepared to document and recommend sanctions for officers that simply made a mistake. This reality makes it especially important that both citizens and police officers perceive that they are receiving procedural justice and fair treatment at every level within the criminal justice system (NJOAG, 2017).

In smaller departments or stand-alone precincts or divisions of larger departments, it has become standard operating procedure for any walk -in complainant to receive personal attention and a documented preliminary interview conducted by the highest-ranking supervisor on duty.

Typically, these interviews are recorded on a form or computer referral field that is forwarded to the designated internal investigator, agency head, or unit (depending on the size of the department and the structural/procedural nature of the internal investigatory process). If immediate action is warranted, current practice requires the ranking supervisor to do so. This is the main reason why a good investigation can improve police-community relationships, and a poorly conducted investigation can damage these relationships (NJOAG, 2017).

Good and Bad Investigations

Distinguishing between a good and bad investigation is important for identifying a comparative measure for all investigations. This is important because it identifies a standard for case investigations. Internal investigations need to be held to the highest agency standards. This imperative will reflect positively on the investigator and their unit, and the agency. Integrity and competency are the key ingredients for success. If the investigation survives external scrutiny, this goes a long way towards investigator, unit, and agency legitimacy.

One way that distinguishes a good investigation from a bad investigation is the timeliness and thoroughness of the investigation. This is especially important when a complainant becomes uncooperative after the initial complaint. It is understood that people can be vindictive and may lie to further their own agenda, but that doesn't mean their allegations aren't truthful. It is the astute investigator that conducts inquiries into all aspects of the allegations, including the complainant and the subject(s).

To conduct a high quality, comprehensive investigation, there are certain recommendations that need to be followed. To begin, the investigator needs to apply what is commonly referred to in forensic investigations as crime scene reconstruction. What sequence of events occurred that resulted in the complaint? To do this, the investigator needs to establish timelines, connections between individuals, and anything that can create a comprehensive picture of what occurred to create this scenario. If the allegation is false, the investigator can establish that relatively quickly since things, events, people don't connect (Gehl, 2017).

Another important aspect to consider is when a complainant becomes less than cooperative or even wishes to withdraw the complaint. There could be a multitude of reasons this is occurring. It does not mean, however, that the allegations didn't occur. The astute investigator should continue to collect information surrounding the allegation, whether in support or not. Only after a comprehensive documentation can the investigator be sure of the veracity of the complaint (NYPD, 2006).

This investigative process requires due diligence from the investigator. Information should be documented in as detailed a manner as possible. The investigator never knows when an insignificant piece of information may become important. This requires steps to be taken in a timely fashion. Information perishes with time and undue delays complicate the investigation and make information collection difficult if not impossible.

These simple guidelines highlight the important aspects of a high-quality investigation. Are the investigators focused on their efforts to obtain the truth? Are they diligent in their investigative activities? Are the case documents detailed, memorializing all aspects of the investigative step? When keeping these questions at the forefront of any investigation, the investigation will reflect high quality efforts and integrity and offer a benchmark for comparison.

In contrast, a bad investigation misses all of the thoroughness required for a proper investigation. One of the major aspects to influence a poor investigation is the timeliness factor. Information and evidence deteriorates with time. The longer one waits, the more difficult it is to obtain a complete picture of events. Memories deteriorate, evidence gets lost, investigative opportunities are missed, which make it improbable to obtain an accurate reconstruction of an incident. The best-case outcome in this instance, is an unsubstantiated finding. This means there is not enough evidence to prove or disprove an allegation. This doesn't help anyone—neither the subject nor the investigator. This is something the investigator wants to avoid (Gehl, 2017).

References

Gehl, R. (2017). *Introduction to criminal investigation: Processes, practices and thinking.* BCcampus.
International Association of Chiefs of Police. (2008). *Police chiefs desk reference: A strategy guide for newly appointed police leaders* (2 edition). Alexandria, VA.
New Jersey, Office of the Attorney General. (2017). *Internal affairs policy & procedures.* https://www.nj.gov/oag/dcj/agguide/internalaffairs2000v1_2.pdf
NYPD. (2006). *Searching for a known perp.* NYC.
U.S. Department of Justice, Office of Community Oriented Policing Services. (2003). *Standards and guidelines for internal affairs: Recommendations from a community of practice.* https://cops.usdoj.gov/ric/Publications/cops-p164-pub.pdf
United Nations Office on Drugs and Crime. (2011). *Handbook on police accountability, oversight and integrity.* United Nations Publication.
Zacarese, L. M. (2016). Leadership in law enforcement: Policing in times of increased scrutiny. *Campus Security Report, 12*(10), 7.

Investigative Perspective; Organizational, Cultural Behavior

Internal affairs investigations are not easy, since they consist of investigating a fellow officer, or another employee in the agency. This quality is compounded by a universal requirement that investigations be conducted dispassionately, without bias. Besides this, the investigator will probably be involved in distasteful work. Or this may have been an involuntarily assignment. Whatever the situation, possessing the proper mindset goes a long way towards completing this task. It benefits the subject of the complaint and makes the investigation more impartial and objective.

Because of the distasteful nature of the work, many investigators bemoan their lot, since they were mandatorily assigned to conduct these investigations. For a period, most newly promoted Sergeants in the NYPD were assigned to the Internal Affairs Bureau as a result of staffing allocation, but also in an effort to enhance their mindfulness and ability to recognize the more subtle forms of misconduct. This was supposed to enable them to quickly overcome the cultural paradigms that can oftentimes prevent newly promoted first-line supervisors from crossing over from the subculture of Police Officers to the subculture of Supervisory personnel. An unpopular policy from the start, it prompted the reluctant investigators to form a common bond with other likeminded investigators. It served no purpose other than contributing to the collective dissatisfaction. It also made the task of managing them that much more difficult. There are some steps that can be taken to reconcile this negativity and thereby make the internal investigative assignment that much easier (Cabral & Lazzarini, 2014).

To begin, these investigations should be viewed as tasks requiring the use of advanced investigatory skills. They should also be seen as performing assigned tasks, which is what work is called. The less the investigator takes it personally as an affront to their crime-fighting skills, the better off they will be.

Allegations come about for a variety of reasons. Complainants can be motivated to engage in counterpunching or have other unscrupulous reasons to lodge personnel complaints. If an investigation is conducted impartially and fairly, the results cannot be disputed. The investigator can do more to assist officers by being the consummate professional than being the angry investigator bemoaning their lot in the police department. Somebody must conduct the investigation and the subject should receive a fair and impartial review of the facts. The investigator should not take this personally and conduct an impartial investigation.

The problem is that the police subculture rejects the entire notion of an internal affairs. It is contrary to the secretive, isolated group that maintains the thin blue line between order and chaos (Caldero et al., 2018). That first line of defense is keeping citizens safe. "Ratting out" fellow officers violates the cultural postulates of teamwork and solidarity, where an affront to one is an affront to all. What is less understood, however, is that a substantiated allegation is more deleterious to the police image than many can imagine (Klockars, et al., 2007).

In the investigator's career, there is little doubt that the investigator will be affected by the actions of others. It is a consequence of being in a group tasked with policing the public. It doesn't matter that the investigator had nothing to do with an incident. The public and media have already formed a collective image of the police that is not readily changed (Maslov, 2015). It is up to the investigator to provide a thorough investigative review of the allegation. In addition, the investigation may have identified someone that may not belong in policing. It could be someone that managed to slip by the extensive background investigation required to be a police officer or succumbed to the innumerable temptations that officers experience every day in their profession. There is also the possibility that the investigator determined that the allegation was unfounded, did not occur, was filed as retaliation or any of many other reasons, and the investigator did their part to exonerate the subject. Handling the case as a professional, and not letting personal feelings cloud personal judgment, go a long way towards completing the investigation.

Underlying Theory of Police Misconduct/Corruption

Police deviance does not occur in a vacuum. As a unique subset within our society, the police subculture operates according to a set of norms, developed through the role defined by the society they operate within. Police officers develop a set of values, unique to the profession, to create a group identity and value system. Values such as group cohesion and teamwork, the ability to maintain a high degree of confidentiality, and the ability to operate at the fringes of society, are the result of the police role within society. The police operate within their own subculture, separate from mainstream society. This has not come without cost (Brooks, 2020).

One of the major consequences of the police subculture has been an ability to rationalize the dehumanization of people. The officer can reconcile, or justify, the treatment of any person as an object. Objects may be tangible, but they are inanimate. As a result, the officer can justify any deviant conduct, based on what Gresham Sykes and David Matza (1957) labeled neutralization techniques. The theory to come out of this was the Neutralization Theory.

These techniques are an attempt to explain how delinquent behavior develops. The authors argue that criminogenic behavior begins with learning the basic values of social decency, but norms contrary to what is learned are developed. These influences result in deviance and create an atmosphere to rationalize the conduct. The justification for the deviance is developed according to the techniques—denial of responsibility, denial of injury, denial of the victim, condemnation of the condemners, and appeal to higher loyalties—that Sykes and Matza offered as a rationale for how juveniles developed into delinquents. The application of this theory to deviant police officers is a natural expansion of the theory to include most deviance, including that committed by police officers.

To begin, police officers already tend to objectify people and dehumanize them. It is easy to explain their misconduct within the constraints of neutralization theory. Denial of responsibility implies that the officer has no choice, they succumb to the social pressures of the subculture. Denial of injury is the extension of the objectification of people. Condemning those that condemn places blame on corruption at the highest levels of society, providing a justification of the officer's misconduct. The appeal to the higher authority is the inviolate police subculture, the Blue Wall (Sluder, et al., 1998).

There are other explanations as well that frame police corruption and misconduct. One of the simplest explanations is individual greed. Whether motivated by inadequate compensation, frustration, or desire, individual greed creates the climate for the officer to balance this perceived inequity. This attitude of, "I'll take my share," is a prime motivator to create the equity in what is considered by the officer a system that is out of balance, favoring the criminals at the expense of the individual officer's livelihood (Sluder et al., 1998).

Another example of what may explain individual corruption is the Rotten Apple Theory (Griffin & Ruiz, 1999). This theory posits that corruption and misconduct is also an individualistic effort, perpetrated by those officers that have slipped through the psychological assessment process. In this instance, their integrity is compromised so that deviant acts are explained away as a failure with integrity. But there is increasing recognition that this conduct may be the consequence of the stressful nature of the work, which provides the impetus towards deviance.

This can be explained under the realm of Environmental Theory, which originated within the nursing field. (Nightingale, 1860). The extension of this theory to the spatial analysis of crime and thereby, police deviance, is done easily. Here, things come together in time and place to provide the elements conducive to deviance. The various theories under this umbrella are considered under the notion that criminality can be understood as the product of environmental, criminogenic factors, and choices are made according to how easy it is to commit the crime.

References

Brooks, D. (2020). The culture of policing is broken. *The Atlantic*. https://www.theatlantic.com/ideas/archive/2020/06/how-police-brutality-gets-made/613030/

Cabral, S., & Lazzarini, S. G. (2014). The guarding the guardians problem: An analysis of the organizational performance of an internal affairs division. *Journal of Public Administration Research and Theory, 25*(3), 797–829.

Caldero, M. A., Dailer, J. D., & Withrow, B. L. (2018). *Police ethics: The corruption of noble cause*. Routledge.

Griffin, C., & Ruiz, R. (1999). Sociopathic police personality: Is it a product of the "Rotten Apple" or the "Rotten Barrel?". *Journal of Police and Criminal Psychology, 14*(1), 28–37.

Klockars, C. B., Ivković, S. K., & Haberfeld, M. R. (2007). *Enhancing police integrity*. Springer.

Maslov, A. (2015). *Measuring the performance of the police: The perspective of the public*. Public Safety Canada. https://www.publicsafety.gc.ca/cnt/rsrcs/pblctns/2015-r034/2015-r034-en.pdf.

Nightingale, F. (1860). *Notes on nursing: What it is and what it is not* (p. 6).

Sluder, R. D., Kappeler, V. E., & Alpert, G. P. (1998). *Forces of deviance: Understanding the dark side of policing* (2nd ed.). Waveland Press.

Sykes, G. M., & Matza, D. (1957). Techniques of neutralization: A theory of delinquency. *American Sociological Review, 22*(6), 664–670. https://doi.org/10.2307/2089195

A Continuum of Incident Classifications

Internal investigators handle a variety of cases, based on a continuum of egregious behaviors. From minor administrative and rules violations, to misconduct, and crimes, internal investigators may find themselves called upon to investigate any one of these incidents. Each of these incidents requires investigative steps in order to be completed properly. Conducting these steps protects the investigator from complaints and goes a long way towards determining exactly what occurred, whatever the complaint.

On the continuum of misconduct and corruption, administrative and rules violations allegations are at the lowest level. Depending on agency procedures, these investigations are usually handled internally within the agency, and if substantiated, involve administrative sanctions (NJOAG, 2017).

At the upper level of the continuum, criminal allegations are much more complex and require district attorney involvement. The most extreme consequence of the substantiated complaint of a serious crime is most often an arrest and prosecution. Of course, this depends on the severity of the allegation, but highlights the importance of conducting a comprehensive, accurate investigation. The importance of this cannot be overstated. The consequences are dire, and the subject of the complaint must receive a professional investigation into the incident.

When criminal complaints are alleged, which may result in the arrest of a police officer, there are two schools of thought regarding the initiation of disciplinary charges. The first and most traditional process suspends any disciplinary investigation until the criminal case is resolved. This is because an internal investigation that includes testimony from the accused officer is often inadmissible in a criminal case. Officers are ordered to cooperate with investigations, and this includes compelled responses to questioning by the designated internal investigators. Therefore, Fifth and Sixth Amendment issues arise; compelled responses to queries posed in this context cannot be introduced at trial. Consequently, administrators must confront the equally distasteful prospect of returning the accused officer to limited duty at full pay, placing the officer on *paid* suspension, or proceeding with the internal investigation with a strategy where unrelated misconduct is uncovered. An example might be investigating the accused officer's personal off-duty comportment and associations. If conduct unbecoming an officer, such as association with known felons or drug users is revealed, and the officer fails a reasonable cause drug screening- many departments have zero tolerance policies that justify termination. The unrelated criminal case can then be expedited (NYPD, 2016).

In the politically charged environment arising from the increasing use of ubiquitous yet unofficial surveillance (i.e., open-source YouTube footage posted and gone viral), police agency heads have been pressured as never before to perform scant, minimal investigations and terminate officers before the criminal process can even begin (Reiner, 2001). Investigators are often caught in the middle of this; pressured to find some way to minimize the connection between the acts of an individual officer or group of officers and the policies and practice of the wider department and executives in charge. This is an awesome responsibility; internal investigations should be impartial and fair to all, yet there is no doubt that political expediency can play a role in outcomes.

Types of Allegations

The law enforcement agency typically identifies the allegations that will be investigated. These can be considered along a continuum of deviance, from minor transgressions to major crimes. Typically, allegations fall into one of three types—administrative, misconduct, or criminal, depending on the severity of the act. Administrative allegations (lateness, improper paperwork, failure to submit required work) usually consist of rules violations. Someone failed to follow policy, which resulted in a transgression. This transgression is usually handled within the Department, through its internal, administrative processes. Sanctions such as loss of time, distasteful assignment, loss of privilege, are typical of this type of transgression. A typical case is where someone neglected, or failed to follow procedure, which resulted in a consequence.

Allegations of misconduct are more serious than administrative violations and carry more severe sanctions. These incidents can include (but are not limited to) allegations of excessive force, unjustified use of firearms, insubordination, and drug use. If these acts are found to constitute a "pattern of practice," then the department itself can be held liable and subject to investigation by the United States Department of Justice, Civil Rights Division (USCOCR, 2000).

At the extreme end of the continuum are the allegations of crimes. Here, the allegation involves an unlawful act, or a harmful act to an individual or society, which is punishable by law. The continuum of crimes goes from violations, through misdemeanors, to felonies, all defined by the attached sanctions. These can be a fine for violations, to incarceration for a year for misdemeanors, to more than a year for felonies. There is an added complexity to the investigation with the statute of limitations for criminal prosecution along with the administrative timelines for internal investigations. Regardless of the level of severity of the allegation, all allegations require the same investigative steps at the outset of the investigation, when the agency is made aware of the allegation. Once these steps are completed, additional steps are determined by the allegation (NJOAG, 2017).

The initial investigation of an incident begins when an allegation comes to the attention of the department. Usually a police supervisor is notified, and while in smaller departments may be screened by a ranking supervisor initially, these allegations should be immediately referred to an appropriate investigator to conduct a more thorough preliminary investigation. In large police department, internal investigations are conducted by a separate bureau or division, complete with its own intake section and investigative resources. Whatever the model used in the agency, it is important that this initial investigation be complete and thorough. Any future investigation can be adversely affected by mistakes or omissions committed through a substandard investigation.

During this initial investigation, the investigative priority is to collect as much information about the incident as possible. Evidence and information are perishable, and it is the investigator's mission to obtain all the information pertinent to the incident (NJOAG, 2017).

Initial Investigations

The initial investigation into an incident occurs when the department becomes aware of the allegation. Whatever the means used to make the agency aware of the allegation, the investigation begins with the receipt of the complaint. A typical intake would consist of someone calling in an allegation of missing property. Maybe the person was arrested and now alleged they were missing some personal property they had before their arrest and processing. It is incumbent on the representative processing the call to collect as much information for the assessment as possible. This would consist of personal and contact information and the details behind the allegation. Times, dates, locations, are all important pieces that must be recorded in the complaint. Remember, the more comprehensive the initial contact, the easier the follow-up investigation will be. There may also be a time factor to consider, which may impact how the investigation is conducted (NYPD, 2016).

The allegation may have occurred a while ago, and there may be a statute of limitations issue, administrative and criminal, with regard to any sanctions. In the case of a crime, the statute of limitations is defined by law. In the case of administrative statutes of limitations, they are defined by the agency. Investigators must begin the process right away, the imperative being able to retrieve evidence that may perish with time. Whether video, witness statements, or records, the evidence may become irretrievable after a certain length of time. This is particularly troublesome when the incident occurred a while ago. There may no longer be any evidence available and can render the investigation all the more difficult, if not impossible. In this instance, only due diligence and perseverance may uncover something that can be enhanced additionally.

Case Assessment and Classification

Whenever the agency receives an allegation that needs to be investigated, there are certain actions that need to be taken to properly identify what category the allegation fits into and the type of ensuing investigation required. The assessment of a complaint is the same for all allegations, which requires classification of the incident and an assessment of the veracity of the complainant and complaint.

The initial assessment begins with evaluating how soon after the incident the complaint was filed. In those cases where a substantial amount of time has lapsed, there may be a question of an administrative statute of limitations, besides the criminal one. When the investigation is warranted, there is the added difficulty of attempting to obtain evidence which may no longer be available. Is the urgency to begin the initial investigation still there? When evaluating the allegation, these considerations should inform whether or not there is the middle of the night notification, or the initial investigation can be started in the morning during normal business hours. What the agency wants to prevent in all cases, however, are allegations that the investigator received the complaint and did nothing about it.

When it is determined that an initial investigation is warranted immediately, an appropriate investigator needs to be assigned. This can be based on assignment or geography, based on the agency's organizational structure. Make sure to document the notification of who was notified of the assignment of the initial investigation and provide all the supporting documents. In this case, the complaint, any intake processing information, and anything else relevant to the incident will need to be readily available for the assigned investigator.

When receiving allegations of misconduct, there are additional steps necessary to determine where in the continuum the allegation fits. This is not needed for criminal allegations because ultimately, the investigation is reviewed by the district attorney for the agency's jurisdiction. Because misconduct allegations involve administrative violations, the investigator needs to assess the evidence and the egregiousness of the allegation. Assess the evidence, the complainant, and witnesses, if any, and the subject. If this is done accurately, the investigator will obtain an accurate evaluation of the complaint and whether the investigation will be fruitful. This does not mean that the investigator can dismiss complaints with poor assessments. All complaints are investigated. The investigator just get a sense of the investigative effort required to complete an investigation (NYPD, 2016).

Typical Investigations and Suggested Investigative Steps-Introduction

The investigator are required to document all investigative activity during an investigation. This provides a permanent record of the incident. It codifies the investigative timeline and offers the evidence in support of a specific disposition (NJOAG, 2017).

One thing to remember when reading or reviewing this section is that all investigations are unique. Each one requires investigative actions not necessarily needed for other similar complaints. There are similarities in all investigations where the complaint is of a similar nature, which require certain, similar steps. What follows is a summary of these typical investigative steps. After outlining what investigative steps must be conducted for the allegation at hand, unique steps are offered, based on the nature of the complaint.

Common Investigative Steps

In all instances the investigator should begin by reviewing the initial investigation, if conducted. This is an important task. Contemporary police best practices require that a ranking officer immediately screen incoming personnel complaints and interview the complainant if possible. This requirement is intended to assure the community that allegations of police misconduct, no matter how seemingly trivial, are taken seriously and investigated accordingly. However, this preliminary screening may have been conducted by a supervisor without investigative skills and/or specialized training, and therefore may be tainted. Hence, the investigator must begin again, reviewing all available evidence, actions taken initially, and the investigator will want to review anything related to the initial complaint. Whether in writing, or called into an intake center, the investigator needs to make sure that all the information was captured correctly, and nothing is missing from the complaint. Listen to any audio recordings and review any video footage that may have been obtained. The purpose of this is to make the investigator familiar with the incident, what investigative steps were completed, and identify what may still be required to complete the thorough investigation of the allegation (NYPD, 2016).

The investigator should contact the complainant within the first several days of receiving the complaint. The purpose of this is twofold. First, to introduce oneself as the investigator and to obtain any additional information that may be required. If the investigator is unable to establish contact with the complainant, the investigator should consider filing a notification within the agency that this individual is wanted for questioning by the investigator's unit. This makes finding the person easier because any police interaction will prompt a notification to the investigator. Make sure to cancel this request at the end of the investigation. It will avoid all sorts of embarrassment (NYPD, 2016).

The investigator needs to canvas for video footage right away. An extensive search of the incident location mut be conducted to see if there are any video cameras that may have captured the incident. Usually, these cameras are intended for security use, but their positioning may be helpful to the investigation. The important thing to keep in mind is that not all video is recorded and if it is, it may not be kept for that long before it is overwritten. This will depend entirely on the complexity of the equipment. In any case, the investigator need to determine if any footage that has investigative value was recorded, and for how long. Based on this finding, the investigator should obtain a copy of the relevant footage by any legal and appropriate means. These systems can be quite complex and require special knowledge of the system to operate. The investigator can always capture a copy of the footage with the investigator's cellphone (NYPD, 2016).

Next, the investigator should obtain and review any 911 or complaint intake recording—emails, letters, etc. The investigator will document exactly what the complainant reported and avoid any transcription issues.

Conduct background checks on the subject. The investigator will need to review the subject's personnel records. Besides reviewing the subject's background information, the investigator needs to check if the subject has a history of similar complaints. While the reasons for filing a complaint are myriad, several similar complaints may warrant additional investigation.

Similar complaints don't automatically establish a pattern but warrant additional scrutiny. It is entirely possible that an officer with numerous arrests collects numerous allegations of missing property. This is not the consequence of any misconduct, but a way for the arrestees to lash out at the officer and the system. These perpetrators know the system and understand that allegations can cause issues for the officer. It is possible that the investigator may be able to establish a criminal association through this review, which is conduct forbidden by most police agencies and must be carefully reviewed. Allegations that are founded have a negative impact on an employee's career, and the investigator must conduct a thorough investigation to establish the facts, which may point towards additional, proactive investigative steps (Thurnauer, 2002).

These proactive steps usually require what is considered an integrity test. An integrity test is a scenario-based incident created by the investigator and based on the allegation, designed to test a target's response. These can be quite complex, but when conducted properly, cannot be distinguished from normal police work and are a good indicator of the subject's professional performance. In the case of law enforcement personnel, the investigator should incorporate a review of the subject's personnel records to determine their pedigree and their history of complaints. The investigator will want to document any history of similar allegations and the dispositions, and any instances where the officer may have triggered an early warning intervention flagging. Note its nature and what if any counseling was offered to the officer. Due to the importance of integrity tests, additional information is provided in the next chapter.

In all instances, in the case of the complainant, the investigator should conduct criminal background checks. In all cases, establish a profile of the person and include it in the investigative case folder. The purpose of this is to provide a broad picture of who the investigator is dealing with. This should be done before the investigator interviews any complainants and witnesses. The investigator will want to know with whom they are dealing. Criminal records, pedigree information, and even a photograph, will serve the investigator well when meeting with complainants.

The complainant may be a serial criminal, but their allegation has validity. When an allegation is serious, the investigator should conduct a thorough background check of the complainant. What the investigator is doing with this background check is identifying a personality typology of the individual. This, in turn, will inform the investigator's tactical response to the interview. Whether, accompanied by additional investigators or choice of interview location. Background information is key to keeping everyone safe and gives the investigator an indication of who the investigator is dealing with. Be careful, though, not to let any negative records influence the investigator's opinions. Maintaining a dispassionate perspective and only collecting relevant facts and information that can be corroborated, should be the investigative philosophy (USDOJ, 2003).

In the investigation into a police officer, the investigator wants to obtain and review any activity records-in greater detail than a simple early warning trigger. When requesting this information, the investigator wants to request a broad range of dates, not just a specific date. The investigator doesn't want to alert the officer that they are the subject of an investigation. However, the courts have recently begun to authorize a much greater array of personnel records as subject to Freedom of Information Law requests than ever before (Boyle & Vullierme, 2018). The investigator certainly doesn't want an attorney representing a complainant to have more knowledge relative to the accused officer's disciplinary record than the investigator does. Once obtained, check whether the record is accurate and complete.

Prepare a letter to the complainant with the final disposition if the investigator's department closes or concludes the investigation. Include the letter in the investigative file but do not forward until final approval from the supervisor in the position to grant this approval.

After an investigation and discipline is warranted, document the preparation of the complaint, and include a copy of the complaint in the investigative file. The investigator will have to record any sanction if any, once the discipline has been adjudicated.

Be aware of any statute of limitation dates, whether criminal or administrative. These dates come up quickly and the investigator doesn't want to be the one to let an important date slip by. Besides being an opportunity for external oversight ridicule, this opens the investigator up to allegations of incompetency and possible punitive sanctions. The investigator should avoid this at all costs. *Eighteen months* is almost universally accepted by many police departments as the administrative statute of limitations for non-criminal complaints, however, be quite clear about the investigator's own department's policies in this regard (NYPD, 2016).

The investigator should interview the complainant again, in person, and within a reasonable amount of time. Best practices suggest an interview within a few days of receiving the complaint. Repeat the questions that were already asked, in order to corroborate the story and make sure that it hasn't changed. The investigator may want to consider asking the complainant (and officer involved or accused) to recount the events backwards, as the FBI has found this to be effective technique in uncovering deception (Hood & Hoffman, 2019).

The investigator will follow general interviewing guidelines which has four objectives:

1. Establish rapport with the person, attempting to put them at ease.
2. Involve the person in the discussion, moving from casual conversation to the specific information that the investigator need.
3. Control the information gathering, while exploiting the individual for all relevant information.
4. Develop rapport with the person being interviewed. Also, mirroring techniques, where the investigator matches voice, tone, breathing, and body posture to the person being interviewed will greatly enhance a successful interaction.

Begin this process at the initial meeting. Put the person at ease with a handshake, a voice and tone that is friendly in nature but businesslike and professional. The investigator is attempting to establish some common ground to facilitate the conversation (Gehl, 2017).

While maintaining this appearance, the investigator will always be alert for potential leads, those bits of information that the investigator can capitalize upon when warranted. It is the investigator's primary responsibility as an investigator to exploit the person of as much relevant information as the investigator can, and to maintain positive control of the information gathering process (Gehl, 2017).

The investigator should record most interviews, remembering not to record district attorneys or other law enforcement when conferring with them, because these conversations can be considered discoverable. Also, some complainants get anxious when they see a recorder. Best practices suggest keeping a digital recorder hidden in a pocket or underneath an investigative notebook goes a long way towards obtaining an accurate interview.

The investigator should also use this opportunity with the complainant to obtain a signature, or medical records if necessary. The investigator can also photograph reports of injuries, or lack thereof. Remember, injuries fade with time. Hence, the importance of documenting quickly and accurately cannot be overstated (Gehl, 2017).

With regard to a photo array, they should be in color. Whether identified or not, specific legal guidelines must be followed in preparing the photo array. The photos should not have any indication who the subject officer is. The complainant needs to review the protos independently, without any hint of suggestion. In fact, recent rulings have mandated double-blinded procedures, where the investigator does not know the order of the photos presented to the complainant or who the actual subject of the investigation may be. This is done by creating three separate arrays, changing the subject's position in each array. These are then placed in nondescript envelopes and the complainant can choose any envelope to review (MPTC, 2015).

If the complainant identified a subject, have them sign and date underneath the photo. If they are not completely sure, the investigator needs to document that as well. Do not have them acknowledge any identification if they are not completely certain.

Having a digital recording of this interaction will go a long way towards protecting the investigator from allegations that the investigator influenced the complainant or somehow suggested or steered them to make a certain selection. It also allows for additional review, as when a question comes up about the interaction with the complainant. Digital records are proof positive of the event.

Proactive Measures

There are times when the investigation requires something more than collecting facts of what occurred. The investigator may want to consider proactive measures in the course of information gathering. Going out and making arrests, or executing dormant warrants, are a way that offers the investigator an opportunity to debrief prisoners. Investigator are apprehending people that may have intimate knowledge of the goings on within a community. Police officers operate in the neighborhoods for their shifts and leave. Residents remain and may be an excellent source of information (USDOJ, 2019). After the investigator makes the arrest, take the time to ask them questions about their knowledge of corruption. While most times the investigator will obtain little of value, there may be times when actionable information is received. It is important to make sure to evaluate and corroborate any statements. People will tell the investigator anything if they perceive any sense of leniency or benefit (USDOJ, 2019). Barring this issue, this may be the only way to gather certain types of information. Of course, this will be determined largely from the nature of the allegations and the level of detail of the investigation.

Administering an Integrity Test

An integrity test is a situation, created and monitored, to determine if the subject is complying with agency policy. There are two types of integrity tests, random and targeted. In a random test, no particular person is targeted. In a targeted test, a particular person is evaluated regarding the allegation, and to determine if there is a pattern of recidivism (DCAF, 2020).

If, during the course of the investigation, it is determined that an integrity test is warranted, the investigator needs to develop a plan to administer the test. Depending on the resources that the investigator has available, these tests can be quite elaborate. The test should be developed to place the subject in a situation like the complaint and monitor how they respond. Too many times, however, the test is transparent to the subject and does not accomplish what it was intended for—verify the subject's integrity. This may be partly the result of the officer's awareness, the awkwardness of the scenario, or even the mannerisms of the undercover role player.

The investigator will need to develop a tactical plan for the scenario. The investigator will assign roles to the available personnel to cover all aspects of the scenario. Everyone needs to know what part in the scenario they will play, whether it be undercover, ghost, medic, recorder, and they all need to understand the scenario, completely. The undercover is the role player and may involve more than one; the ghost maintains constant surveillance of the undercover; the medic provides first aid and transportation to the hospital; the recorder captures a video recording of the scenario with the targeted subject. The investigator will really have only one attempt at this, hence the imperative that it be rehearsed and conducted properly.

Once concluded, there are several results of a completed integrity test:

- A Pass occurs when the subject responded and handled the test according to agency guidelines. In this instance, no violation was observed. A Fail occurs when the subject responded and committed a crime or misconduct when handling the test.
- An Attempt is documented when the scenario was in place, but there was no response by the targeted subject (i.e.., someone else handled the assignment).
- An Inconclusive finding occurs when the scenario was in place and the subject responded, but the subject did not become engaged in the scenario.
- A Procedural Deficiency occurs when the subject handled the incident but committed procedural violations. This is usually the case when the subject didn't follow agency guidelines when handling the incident.
- A Supervisory Deficiency occurs when a supervisor failed to follow the supervisory guidelines regarding the incident.
- A Criminal Deficiency occurs when the subject, or someone else involved in the scenario, committed a crime, larceny being the most common (NYPD, 2016).

At the conclusion of the integrity test, the investigator needs to conduct a debriefing with the team to see what went well, what didn't go so well, and how things can be improved for future tests. Make sure to incorporate these observations into future scenarios.

References

Boyle, M., & Vullierme, J. C. (2018). *A brief introduction to investigative interviewing: A practitioner's guide*. Council of Europe.

DCAF. (2020). *Police integrity testing*. Geneva Centre for Security Sector Governance. https://dcaf.ch/sites/default/files/publications/documents/DCAF_Brief_Police_Integrity_Testing_Jan2021_final_ENG_0.pdf

Gehl, R. (2017). *Introduction to criminal investigation: Processes, practices and thinking*. BCcampus.

Hood, M. B., & Hoffman, L. J. (2019). Current state of interview and interrogation. *FBI Law Enforcement Bulletin*.

References

Municipal Police Training Council. (2015). *Identification procedures: Photo arrays and line-ups model policy.* NY State Division of Criminal Justice Services.

New Jersey, Office of the Attorney General. (2017). *Internal affairs policy & procedures.* https://www.nj.gov/oag/dcj/agguide/internalaffairs2000v1_2.pdf

NYPD. (2016). *Internal affairs bureau procedural guide.* NYC.

Reiner, R. (2001). *The politics of the police.* Oxford University Press.

Thurnauer, B. (2002). Internal affairs: Practice and policy review for smaller departments. *Police Chief, 69*(10), 73, 76, 78, 79, 81, 82.

U.S. Department of Justice, Office of Community Oriented Policing Services. (2003). *Standards and guidelines for internal affairs: Recommendations from a community of practice.* https://cops.usdoj.gov/ric/Publications/cops-p164-pub.pdf

U.S. Department of Justice, Office of Community Oriented Policing Services. (2019). *Law enforcement best practices: Lessons learned from the field.* https://cops.usdoj.gov/ric/Publications/cops-w0875-pub.pdf

United States Commission on Civil Rights. (2000). *Revisiting who is guarding the guardians? A report on police practices and civil rights in America.* https://www.ojp.gov/pdffiles1/bja/249021.pdf

Interviewing the Subject

The investigator has exhausted all investigative leads and has a solid understanding of events. Then, it is time to interview the subject of the complaint. During this interview, the subject should be allowed to explain their version of events. Remind them that the final decision as to degree of blameworthiness or action taken is not the investigator's purpose or responsibility. Those decisions are made at higher echelons within the agency. This allows the subject to explain their actions and confirms that the properly identified subject did or did not commit the allegation.

Before conducting the interview, there are a few things that the investigator should keep in mind. If the allegation is criminal in nature, the investigator needs to make sure that the District Attorney will waive any prosecution (NJOAG, 2017). Many agencies compel their personnel to answer questions in an administrative hearing with the caveat that criminal prosecution is waived. If the waiver is not granted, then the investigator cannot interview the subject. As previously noted, the interview then becomes compelled testimony and is inadmissible in court (Nisenson, n.d.).

The investigator also needs to determine whether the subject is aware of the allegation or not. This condition requires a slightly different investigative response. Your investigative strategy will be determined by whether the subject knows about the allegation. If the subject is aware of the allegation, any interviews will likely elicit a denial and be a waste of time. In instances where the subject is not aware of the allegation, an interview may or may not be warranted. This will depend on the investigative findings. For example, a finding that the allegation is unfounded will not require an interview. In this instance, the investigation is closed, and the subject need not be made aware that the investigation was even conducted (NYPD, 2016).

At the hearing, if held, the investigator need to follow the investigator's agency's policies concerning interviewing agency employees (NJOAG, 2017). The investigator will have to make sure the recording equipment is working by conducting a test of the recording equipment. This test should consist of recording the date and time, the investigative case number, the identity of the investigator, and where the test is being conducted. This test will precede the actual recorded interview and becomes part of the investigative folder. At the actual hearing, the investigator needs to document the date, time, and location of the hearing. All persons present need to identify themselves by name and affiliation for the recording. Remember, this is a permanent record of the subject's statements regarding the incident, and the investigator needs to make sure that all of the recording equipment is functioning correctly. The last thing the investigator wants is for a malfunction to prevent the proper recording of the hearing. To have to repeat it is a problem; it wastes departmental funds, changes the dynamics of the interview, and is something to be avoided at all costs.

Most agencies compel their personnel to answer questions posed by a supervisor truthfully, and to the best of their ability. The Fifth Amendment applies to criminal trials and any statements made at an agency hearing cannot ordinarily be used at a criminal trial. Garrity rights for law enforcement assures this (Nisenson, n.d.). Subjects must be aware, however, whether the interview is part of an internal investigation or a criminal one, where Miranda applies. Because of the complex nature of interviewing subjects, investigators want to ask questions specifically directed and narrowly related to the subject's official duties with regard to the allegation.

During the interview, the investigator will want to maintain a professional demeanor. Questions should follow a natural progression, from demographic information to specifics of the allegation. The investigator must maintain a professional demeanor, keeping it impersonal, withholding any opinion or derogatory comments. It is the investigator's job to obtain the subject's statements regarding the incident and to ask clarifying questions, if needed.

These interviews are normally conducted at the conclusion of the investigation. All investigative steps have been conducted, and the subject's statements are required to corroborate the facts collected. That is why the agency compulsion to answer questions truthfully is so important. Any attempt at lying or distorting the truth may result in administrative sanctions, including termination (NYPD, 2016).

One final note concerning interviewing subjects, is where they should be conducted. A separate room, away from general office activity is preferred. The room should contain a conference table and some chairs. The walls should be bare, to minimize distractions. A room without windows, or covered windows is preferred, also to minimize distractions. The room should have a professional, serious quality. These suggestions will assist the investigator maintain the seriousness of the investigation, especially when the employees know each other.

References

New Jersey, Office of the Attorney General. (2017). *Internal affairs policy & procedures*. https://www.nj.gov/oag/dcj/agguide/internalaffairs2000v1_2.pdf

Nisenson, A. (n.d.). *Garrity rights for law enforcement officers*. United Public Employees Service Union. https://www.upseu.org/cops/GARRITY%20RIGHTSLawEnforcement.pdf

NYPD. (2016). *Internal affairs bureau procedural guide*. NYC.

Occupational Crimes Specific to the Role of Police Officers-Introduction

These next sections are investigative steps specific to the listed allegation. It is important to follow the steps identified in the section, Common Investigative Steps, because these steps are common to all investigations. Now, the investigator should incorporate the additional steps into the investigation. Where warranted, additional clarification is provided.

These allegations tend to be part of the occupational crimes specific to the roles of police officers. In their daily activities, officers are confronted with a variety of situations where misconduct and corruption can occur. Daily policing is rife with these opportunities. For those personnel in the profession that are honorable and have integrity, they can resist these opportunities. For others, who succumb to temptation, are why these investigations occur at all. In the list of specific allegations, some typical investigative steps are offered, along with those steps unique to the allegation. These steps are identified from the investigations into similar allegations and are typical steps required for a comprehensive and complete investigation.

Missing Property Allegations

Traditionally, a missing property complaint is the most frequent type of allegation that the investigator will encounter. These cases typically involve a subject who is accused of stealing someone's property. They are the result of an encounter with the police and the complainant alleged something was taken. Most of the time the allegation involves money, but other items can be involved. For example, a homeless person once alleged that his Rolex watch was stolen by the police. A video canvas revealed that plainclothes officers interacted with the person. The video captured them arriving, getting out, and confronting the person. At this point, the interaction is out of the camera frame, but eventually, the investigator can see the officers returning to their vehicle and leaving. The complainant alleged that his watch was stolen, but additional canvas for video captured the individual showing the watch to another person, after the alleged interaction with the police. He was clearly in possession of what he alleged was taken. When confronted, he confessed to making the false allegation against the officers. This anecdote came from the author's own experiences as a team leader, conducting internal investigations. It was satisfying to note that a false allegation was exposed, and officers were protected from a false allegation.

Another common complaint is the allegation that money was taken during a police encounter. This encounter may result in an arrest, in which all prisoner property is documented upon arrival at the police station, or the individual is released. These allegations are difficult to investigate, due to the lack of evidence. Unless there are bank accounts and receipts to corroborate the funds, substantiating this is extremely difficult. Of course, canvassing for corroborating evidence (witnesses, video) helps clear these investigations (NJOAG, 2017).

Regardless of the type of property, or from where it was taken, missing property allegations require certain, unique investigative steps. When looking into this incident, an initial investigation will have been completed during the complaint intake process, and it was determined that additional investigation into the incident is warranted. The following steps are part of the investigation into the allegation and need to be incorporated into the case folder:

- Review the Initial Complaint and Investigation: Make sure to review all complaint information and all records of an initial investigation. Write a summary of this initial review and add the initial investigation as an attachment to this review.
- Interview the Complainant and Witnesses: The assigned investigator needs to verify how the property was taken. In the case of missing money, the investigator will need to determine how the person obtained the money, and how they knew how much was taken. In this instance, receipts (bank, restaurant, etc.) are important because it could change the amount of money that the person thought they had. Let people speak freely. All of this needs to be recorded and the recording and any evidence needs to be attached to the investigative report of the interview.
- Determining the person's travel route will help the investigator to pursue additional investigative leads, whether for witnesses or video recordings of the incident.
- Besides attempting to verify that the property existed, the investigator will need to ask clarifying questions about the property. Attempt to determine why the person had the property with them. How much was the property worth? Where did they initially get it from? Why did they have it? What occurred during their encounter with the police? If the complainant admits to lying, the investigator has probable cause to arrest. There is an inherent problem with making an arrest that the investigator needs to consider. If the complaint lied this time, it does not mean that they will lie the next time and every time thereafter. There is a fine line between preventing false complaints and promoting truthfulness. In any case, make sure to have supervisory approval before effecting an arrest. If the arrest is appropriate, process it in the normal fashion.

Missing Property Allegations

- Canvasses for Video: Refer to the section on Common Investigative Steps for explanation and clarification.
- Review subject's personnel profile: The investigator will need to identify all personnel that had access to the property (NYPD, 2016).

If the property consisted of jewelry, electronics, or the like, the investigator should check the website, LeadsOnline, to see if the subject or complainant sold the missing property. LeadsOnline is a law enforcement technology resource to locate missing items (LeadsOnline, 2022). Businesses (pawn brokers) are typically required to report their transactions to law enforcement and this service becomes a repository for these transactions, facilitating investigations. The investigator must register to access the LeadsOnline resources. These resources are for law enforcement only. Make repeated searches and document them, during the investigation. Just because the investigator didn't find anything in one instance, it doesn't mean it won't eventually turn up.

LeadsOnline has expanded their services to include investigative tools that detect deception, with their Statement Analyzer, searching eBay, providing forensic sketches, a system for maintaining personal property records, and thwarting thefts of metals, and even a cold case function where the case investigator is alerted if a relevant hit is found.

If the property consisted of a cash-related item (credit or debit card, money order), the investigator needs to contact the company to determine if the card was used after the alleged incident. If so, respond to the location and look for video or transaction records.

If the property was a telephone, the investigator needs to gather usage records, also after the alleged incident. If the complainant can access usage records online, great. Have them provide the investigator with a copy of these usage records for the dates covering the alleged theft and thereafter. If the complainant cannot provide the investigator with these records, the investigator will have to subpoena this information. An administrative subpoena should suffice, since the investigator is only accessing contact numbers and no private, personal information. Cellular providers deal with this constantly and have excellent resources available to the investigator. Remain cognizant of timeframes, though. Records get deleted to make room for new records and the investigator doesn't want to miss information because the request was delayed, and records were lost.

If the property consists of a money order, determine if there is a tracking number. The investigator can then contact the issuing company and determine if it was used, and where. If cashed, canvas the location for video, records, and any information to identify who cashed the money order.

If the missing property is related to the execution of a search warrant, the investigator should obtain a copy of the tactical plan. Not everyone involved had access to the property and will automatically become a subject. The plan will identify those that entered the location. Even then, agency procedure will help narrow the list of subjects. Not all tactical officers go through a person's pockets or open drawers.

Fraud

A representative example of this type of crime is when an officer uses the credit card to make unauthorized purchases. The following anecdote, experienced by the author, typifies this type of allegation. Officers receive a call to investigate a possible dead person. Upon arrival, they found the person deceased, apparently of natural causes, and living alone. They searched the scene to secure any valuables and one officer found a credit card, not expired, and took it. Several days later, the officer made a large purchase online, in this instance a piece of jewelry which cost several thousand dollars, and had the item shipped to an address, other than their residence. The shipping address belonged to a relative. The only reason the police were made aware of the allegation was because family members of the deceased noticed the transaction, after the date of death and reported it. It was the family's due diligence that brought this to light and helped the Department rid itself of an opportunistic employee.

Association with Criminals

Officers develop vast networks of friends and acquaintances beyond their coworkers in the police department. Some of these associations may involve criminals. This is a complex typology, because the term criminal may mean current, or former, relative, or not. If the criminal, i.e., someone with a criminal record, is a relative, the investigator has a particularly sensitive situation. The officer may have integrity and cannot choose their relatives. In this instance, the investigation should concentrate on how involved the officer is with the relative. The investigation should encompass a phone records review and surveillances to determine any association. If none is established, a periodic review may be warranted to make sure there is no corruption or misconduct evident. These investigations must be kept confidential, to make sure the officer is not stigmatized as a criminal (NJOAG, 2017).

The other instance is when an officer is actively engaged in corruption with criminals. In a specific jurisdiction, many years ago, a warrant executed on a specific street always yielded negative results. No matter what the officers did to ensure a solid investigation into crimes on the street, when the warrant was executed, they came up empty handed. It turned out the officer assigned to that specific beat was accepting bribes for information on the dates the warrants were being executed. Since this area was known for its extensive trade in drugs, the money involved was substantial. In this instance, the officer sold his integrity for some supplemental income. To substantiate the allegation, an integrity test, targeting the beat officer was conducted.

Should the investigation reveal corruption or misconduct, then the investigator should proceed with a criminal referral. This involves a consultation with the district attorney, where the full investigation is shared to determine if criminal charges should be preferred. The investigator needs to follow the recommendations and suggestions resulting from this conferral.

Planting/Padding Evidence (Flaking) Allegations

This type of allegation consists of evidence being illegally associated with an individual in order to increase the severity of charges. The investigator will want to interview any co-defendants or perpetrators held in the same cell to determine what they heard or saw. Make sure to interview prisoners separately and ensure all security procedures are followed to prevent the potential for an escape (Heffernan & Kleinig, 2004).

The investigator needs to obtain copies of all court-related documents. This file should contain everything from the initial stop and arrest, through processing and arraignment, and all court appearances. Documents should include and are not limited to, complaint and arrest reports, property invoices, supporting depositions, court documents, and officer activity records.

The investigator will want to check for inconsistencies or things that just don't add up. Catching these discrepancies is facilitated by maintaining a complete and current knowledge of the investigation. Make sure to review all relevant documents before conducting any interviews. The investigator that knows the case, can use the interview to substantiate or corroborate investigative facts. Afterwards, the investigator will need to confer with the district attorney. Since this allegation often involves perjury, the investigator will require expert legal guidance to conduct the investigation.

An important part of the investigation is to monitor all court appearances. The investigator needs to be present so that they can capture when the perpetrator makes a statement. Was there an admission of guilt? Was a plea negotiated? What was the disposition of the case? These are all questions that need to be answered and incorporated into the investigative case folder. The investigator will also need to inform police executive of the results of any courtroom proceedings right away.

Narcotics Allegations

These types of allegations involve illegal substances. They encompass the continuum of unauthorized possession and ingestion to involvement in the illegal trade. Given the current extensive misuse of opioids, this allegation is particularly troubling because it may consist of a legitimate prescription, but excessive overuse . Although there are exceptions due to union negotiations, illegal drug use is prohibited conduct. No agency wants the liability of having a drug abusing officer involved in a highly charged media event, such as a shooting. Illegal drug use by officers is covered more completely in the next section, Drug Use Allegations (Kleinig, 2012).

Besides the typical investigative steps of reviewing phone records and conducting surveillances, the investigator will want to review the subject's personnel application for any derogatory information. The investigator is looking for previous arrests, admissions of drug usage, family arrest history, and anything else that supports the allegation. The investigator should also look for what may not have been documented in the application, which could indicate deception.

In certain instances, the investigator will want to conduct a full audit of the subject's agency computer usage. Did the subject access databases and obtain records not related to their work function? It is this question that should guide the review of usage records.

Check with detention facilities to determine if the subject made calls, visits, or contributed to an inmate's commissary account. An online check will provide information on inmate whereabouts.

Conducting extensive computer checks are required with this type of allegation. Besides the standard checks, conducted for all investigations and listed in the section on Common Investigative Steps, these checks comprise anything related to narcotics intelligence and enforcement. Agency databases should be reviewed first, along with local, state, and national databases. The intent is to identify a connection with the subject and the allegation.

Check with the local police department where the subject lives. Usually, the investigator will want to establish contact with their internal investigator to act as a liaison. Agencies usually give out information on a need-to-know basis. This can be problematic if they don't know the investigator. Establishing a liaison will make the process easier.

An extensive social media check will be required. Many agencies have accounts with fake identities to facilitate access. This allows the investigator to submit a friend request in order to access these sites. Much information can be obtained from these sites. Understand, however, these reviews can result in new, additional allegations. Incorporate any relevant information into the investigative file.

Surveillances on the subject and any identified associates will also have to be conducted. These are typically difficult, because investigators don't conduct these often and most times, the subject of the surveillance is in law enforcement. Careful planning and proper use of resources will go a long way towards conducting successful surveillances. Document the surveillance with video or photographs. Make sure though, that other law enforcement units are not conducting operations in the area of the surveillance. This is part of planning the surveillance and a computer check should indicate if addresses or individuals are the targets of other investigations (NJOAG, 2017).

Conduct an analysis on relevant phone records to identify the target number and most frequently called number. This analysis will identify a pattern, association, or not. Remember, subpoenas will be required for subscriber information, and these take time. The investigator will have to plan accordingly (PLN, n.d.).

A review of the subject's financial records is also required. The purpose is to establish spending patterns and identify possible illicit income. This can be corroborated through surveillances which can help the investigator to identify a lifestyle lived beyond the subject's means.

Determine if other units are investigating the same individuals. Since this check should have been done already before conducting the surveillances, this will be easy. If there are additional investigations, determine if the subjects in these cases are the same as the current investigation. When dealing with these other units, the investigator do not want to disclose the fact that the investigator are conducting a similar investigation. Confidentiality is paramount and will prevent the investigation from being compromised (NJOAG, 2017).

Once the investigation is completed and an administrative hearing is warranted, the investigator needs to make sure that the subject was directed to abstain from contact, or otherwise associate with a known criminal. This must be documented in the investigative folder. If there ever is a future investigation of a similar nature, this record will become important. It could result in discipline for failing to comply with an order from a superior.

In the case of a family member, the investigator just documents the relationship as intelligence and closes the file. The investigator may not even want to conduct an administrative hearing. What purpose would it serve? A hearing would be warranted in instances when the investigation determined the association is a family member and criminal activity was determined. This would occur after a periodic review of the officer, to include records checks and surveillances.

Drug Use Allegations

One of the first things to do after completing the common investigative steps is to review the subject's drug screening history. List the dates of the screening and the results.

Along with the drug screening history, the investigator will want to review any integrity testing history, along with those results.

Surveillance on the subject should be conducted. Good times for these surveillances are on days off, on paydays, birthdays, and holidays. As part of the surveillance plan, the investigator will want to check bridge or highway toll records, if any, and any available license plate readers. The investigator want to see when the subject travelled and where. Don't forget the importance of area license plate readers (NJOAG, 2017).

If there are parking tickets identified in the investigation, check the addresses in the area for any identified drug activity. This can be accomplished through computer checks, but site visits provide context and should not be discounted.

Searching through the subject's garbage, if legally permissible, is also recommended. Remember, garbage on a subject's property is off limits. Placed outside the curtilage is fair game. The investigator will want to grab it secretly and take it to a location, preferably inside, as in a garage, where the investigator can systematically pick through it with rakes and shovels. If the investigator find evidence of contraband, recover it, and process it as evidence (NJOAG, 2017).

In cases where the investigation is completed with an unsubstantiated finding, the investigator may want to revisit the investigation after a period of time, say 6 months, or whatever agency policy dictates. If there is drug use occurring, the new investigation may uncover evidence of the misconduct or corruption.

Part of these types of investigations involves integrity tests conducted with contraband or money. These are extremely difficult to do well, and careful planning and preparation is mandatory. When conducted properly, the subject is ignorant to the test, and becomes a good indicator of a subject's conduct.

There is also agency drug screening available. This will involve decision-making well above a typical investigator's paygrade but is a viable option when all other investigative avenues have been exhausted. This type of testing would also involve legal consultation to avoid possible entrapment issues (NJOAG, 2017).

Drug screening usually comes in two forms—urinalysis, or hair samples. Urinalysis provides a recent history, although only a relatively short timeline of possible usage. The hair sample provides a much longer timeline but takes some time to become noticeable and will not necessarily capture any recent usage. A combination of the two provides the most complete picture of possible contraband usage, because there is no gap in time (Uritox, 2022).

The agency should have a contract in place with a reputable drug screening facility. Since chain of custody and quality control are of paramount importance, a carefully designed policy must be in place to negate the potential for a false positive.

At the conclusion of the investigation, when the allegation is unfounded or unsubstantiated, in most cases, the investigator will not conduct an administrative hearing. This will only alert the subject to the investigation and would compromise future investigative efforts. A periodic review would be appropriate, if needed.

Drug Screening Failure

Drug screening is a carefully controlled process. Whether urine or hair, three samples are usually collected.

The first is tested and if positive, the test is conducted on a second sample.

The third sample is reserved for the subject to test at their own expense. All evidence is strictly controlled to maintain chain of custody, with the subject signing and initialing everywhere confirming the sample is theirs and was collected properly (NYPD, 2016).

In these cases, the investigator needs to obtain any drug screening documents, right away. In the case of prescription drug cases, obtain all medical documents related to the issuance of the prescription. This would include work-related reports of injuries, medical treatment, and evaluation. In the case of steroid cases, consult the physician who determined that steroid use was authorized (NJOAG, 2017).

Obtain and review any drug screening history and include it in the file. Check for narcotics-related activity involving identified individuals, locations, and vehicles. If other agencies need to be contacted, make all effort to consult with their internal investigators, if they have them. If not, a supervisor is preferred. Other internal investigators understand the internal affairs perspective and will be in a position to facilitate a request for information.

The investigator should also review any integrity testing history, if conducted. If so, determine when it was conducted, what was involved, whether the test was targeted or random, and the results.

Since these instances involve being relieved from duty or suspended pending termination of employment in many cases, the investigator needs to consult agency attorneys. They will guide the investigator in the preparation of the paperwork involved and preparation of administrative charges against the subject.

Once the subject has been relieved from duty, the investigator can request that they resign. This helps the subject because all that is listed in personnel records is that they resigned. If the subject is terminated, that information is available for sharing with future employers conducting a reference check.

Police Officer-Involved DWI Arrests

The first thing to determine is if there are any injuries involved. If so, determine if blood was drawn from the subject. The investigator needs to contact the district attorney to obtain a subpoena or warrant for the blood. In those cases where blood was not drawn, determine if the district attorney will prepare the warrant. Time is of critical importance in these incidents. The longer any delays, the less reliable the BAC level (NJOAG, 2017).

The following steps are typical of this allegation:

- Contact a hospital administrator and request that they preserve the blood. Inform them that a warrant or subpoena is being prepared. Collecting blood is part of normal hospital routine, but it is good to let the hospital know that the subpoena is being prepared.
- Determine where the subject came from—bar, restaurant, party, etc. the investigator will want to obtain copies of receipts and interview patrons and bartenders. In the case of a party, there will be plenty of witnesses to interview.
- Canvas for video, from the location the subject frequented, possible travel routes, and location of any stop and apprehension.
- Interview any responding units as witnesses. This is very important, since responding officers must be included in any and all official correspondence, and if possible, should each file a supplemental incident account. They will be reluctant to become involved except under circumstances where they see no choice. The interviews should be conducted under the guidelines of an administrative hearing, with all the rights and privileges available. They would be listed as witnesses in the investigation.

- Recover the vehicle and safeguard it as evidence and possible forfeiture. Search the vehicle and consult with a district attorney if the search becomes more than an inspection of the interior.
- Consult with the district attorney because this is a criminal matter. Be available for any assistance they may require.

Based on investigative findings and agency policy, the subject may be relieved from duty. When this occurs, obtain and safeguard all department property (NYPD, 2016).

Conduct the administrative hearing after the criminal trial has been adjudicated. Remember, part of the benefit to an administrative hearing is that nothing can be used against the subject in a criminal trial. Consult with the district attorney and be guided by their advice.

Domestic Incidents Involving Police Officers

The Lautenberg Amendment to the Gun Control Act of 1968 prohibited the possession of firearms of persons convicted of domestic misdemeanors. This is of particular relevance to police officers since their employment depends on being authorized to possess and carry firearms. This proscription makes it important that the investigation of domestic violence incidents be conducted properly and correctly (USDOJ, 2020).

First and foremost, make sure the victim receives medical attention, if needed, and they are safe from further aggression. This requires the investigator to evaluate the scene for any potential harmful threats, the history of incidents and the potential for future violence, which includes the location of the primary aggressor. Investigators are dealing with trained, possibly armed employees and safety for everyone is a primary concern.

Whether or not the disputants are together, or one has departed, the investigative steps don't deviate. The investigator is still required to capture the same information but may have to add additional steps to locate the alleged offender. Timeliness is key, as it is in all investigations. It is of particular importance here, because of the potential for a misdemeanor conviction. The investigator must make sure to gather perishable evidence quickly. Evidence deteriorates, memories become faulty, stories change with time. The investigator must maintain due diligence, but with a professionalism, compassion, and empathy towards all involved (Gehl, 2017).

During the initial contact, if the investigator feels they are hindering the interview, have another investigator conduct the interviews. Assume the supporting role of gathering evidence, conducting canvasses, or steps that keep the investigator not involved from the interviews. The last thing the investigator needs is a complaint from someone that is already fraught with emotion.

An important step that should be conducted with all investigations involving interviews, is to conduct background checks of those involved. If additional people are interviewed at the scene, and background checks were not conducted, do so as soon as possible and incorporate these into the investigative file. It is important to be cognizant of the histories of all parties identified in the complaint. It provides the investigator with a proper perspective and awareness of potential safety issues.

The investigation begins as the investigator approaches the scene. Document what the investigator observed arriving at the incident location. What are conditions outside? Inside? What vehicles are in the vicinity of the location? Document the license plates. What does the investigator hear upon arrival? After the investigator has documented the incident scene and surrounding area, begin to focus on the victim. What is their current condition? Are they intoxicated or sober? Where are the involved parties positioned at the incident location?

Once this preliminary, contextual information, is gathered, begin the interviews. These should be conducted in private, out of earshot of others. In the highly charged atmosphere of a domestic violence incident, and both the victim and primary aggressor are still there, the investigator and their partner should begin conversations in sight of each other, with the involved persons' backs to each other (USDOJ, 2020). Conduct these conversations in areas that are relatively safe, where the potential for grabbing something that can be used as a weapon is minimized. Make sure to record everything. It will probably have to be done discretely, since people are generally nervous to have their statements recorded. Also, make sure to determine where the officer's firearms are. They will probably need to be secured at a later time.

The list of people to interview consists of the victim, and primary aggressor, any .witnesses (they may be children), and the caller to the emergency response system. When identifying people to interview, canvassing the neighbors should be conducted. They may have heard or seen something relevant to the investigation.

In the interviews, begin with a comprehensive description of the incident and any past offenses. This is important because a careful, comprehensive documentation now prevents changing the story or even recanting it later. Obtain the victim's attitudes on the incident's disposition. What is their desired outcome for this? This is important to determine since it hints at their willingness to testify during a possible future trial. Make sure to obtain a signed and dated statement of the domestic incident. These forms are typically part of domestic violence paperwork which offer contacts for shelters and other community services.

Make sure to photograph all involved parties, in addition to any sustained injuries and the scene. Capture enough images to provide a comprehensive documentation of the incident. After a few days, take follow up photographs of any injuries to document healing progression. These are important for context of the level of violence experienced (USDOJ, 2020).

Obtain and review any 911 calls. Make sure to add the actual call and any printouts that were generated because of the call. Obtain signatures for the release of medical records and obtain them. Try to obtain approval for any history of treatment for violence and obtain those documents. If an ambulance was dispatched, the investigator should obtain those records. Also, include any Domestic Incident Reports, Protection Orders, and police complaint reports. All these records are important for the investigation because they provide a historical context for the involved parties.

Gather and document any additional evidence relevant to the incident. Is there damage at the location, as the result of the violence? Does anyone else have injuries? If the evidence can't be removed and taken into police custody, make sure to take photographs. Make sure to follow the policies and guidelines of the agency in processing crime scenes (Gehl, 2017).

Force Incidents

Of all the types of misconduct and corruption, force complaints tend to garner the most media attention and become politically charged extremely quickly. That is why the investigation into this allegation must be done expeditiously, comprehensively, and properly. The fallout from a poor investigation will have negative consequences for all involved, from the investigator to the jurisdictional political leaders (Cuncic, 2022).

First and foremost, is to classify the complaint according to a force continuum. The continuum consists of minor use of force on one side of the continuum continuing to deadly, lethal force on the other side. This section concentrates on the most extreme aspect of force—lethal use, resulting in a serious injury or fatality. Lesser levels of force allegations can be investigated according to the standards of all investigations—conducting interviews, canvassing for video evidence, reviewing records. The incident involving use of deadly force requires the foregoing steps but an added requirement of being conducted as soon as possible after the incident (Cunningham, 2021).

There is no one size fits all set of guidelines to follow in these incidents, but there are specific investigative actions that can be taken which common to all force investigations, that will ensure the investigation meets all of the requirements of a professional, high-quality investigation. The following guidelines will focus on the deadly use of force investigations, since these are the most serious types of force incidents (NJOAG, 2017).

As soon as possible after the incident, it is imperative that the investigator implements a multi-pronged investigative plan. This multi-pronged approach requires gathering information from the incident location and any hospitals, along with the records checks of all involved. Most importantly, is to proceed to the scene and begin the process.

At the scene, the investigator should obtain information from any crime scene investigators, if the agency has this office within the organizational chart, or detectives, which would include their case number and names. Let them do their work but obtaining a preliminary interpretation of the crime scene will assist in focusing the internal investigative efforts. This information will not the final interpretation of events, but it can provide a focal point on where to focus factfinding efforts.

Provided with this preliminary information, the investigator will need to begin interviewing any witnesses, police and civilian. The purpose is to verify and confirm which officers were involved in the deadly force incident. Make sure to document the date and time and names of all persons that were interviewed. When interviewing civilians, document their names and residence addresses and what they were doing at the time of the incident. Let them speak freely about what they saw and heard, making sure to record the conversation. Based on the author's personal experiences in many cases, this needs to be done surreptitiously. Apparently, recorders tend to make people nervous. Be cognizant of any agency and jurisdictional regulations on recordings and make sure to follow them. In many areas, knowledge of the recording by one person is satisfactory. In the case of interviewing officers, the investigator may have to be do this later in a formal setting, complete with union and legal representation. At the very least, obtain name and contact information of witness officers for the interview.

Canvass for any video surveillance that may have captured the incident. This can be difficult and time-consuming depending on the day. It requires investigators to review footage to determine field of view first, then if anything was recorded. Given the variety of surveillance technology and whether surveillance is recorded, makes the task challenging. There is a large variety of technology, not all people understand how to operate these systems, and some systems are not recorded. Others are retained for a finite period. That is why this is such an important investigative task and must be started right away. All locations where video was reviewed needs to be documented and positive results need to be added to the investigative folder. Remember, taking a video of a video with a smartphone will work.

At the hospital, if needed, the investigator needs to obtain names of everyone involved in the incident, from ambulance technicians to attending physicians. The investigator may not be able to interview everyone immediately, but proper documentation will facilitate any future interviews. This information is important to obtain all relevant medical records. Understand that the investigator might have to obtain a warrant for these records and the more information that the investigator has, the easier the consultation with investigative district attorneys will be. Most hospitals have a liaison that can assist with obtaining relevant information. Make sure to contact them quickly, so they are in a better position to assist with the investigation.

The administrative tasks involved with the lethal use of force incident are numerous. They must be done however, to ensure important information is not lost. To begin, the involved firearm needs to be obtained and sent to a lab for ballistic analysis. The firearm will need to be examined for gunshot residue and an exemplar round will need to be obtained and invoiced as evidence. If the officer is to return to work right away, a replacement firearm will need to be issued. A standard letter indicating the reason for the loan is usually all that is required.

Relevant incident records need to be reviewed. All records from the emergency dispatch center need to be obtained. This involves the initial calls and subsequent dispatch of emergency services. Background checks need to be completed of all involved officers and involved civilians, interviewed officers and civilians, and incorporated into the investigative file. This can be substantial and require much effort but must be completed.

The aforementioned steps are typical of lethal force incidents and should be conducted in all instances. Understand, however, they may not be all inclusive. Every incident is unique and may require additional steps (NJOAG, 2017).

Whatever the case, a final requirement is to create a report that documents the incident and subsequent investigation. This report will be substantial, since it should be a stand-alone document that provides all required information. Many people will review this, and it is imperative that the report be accurate and reflect a professional investigation.

One final thought on this type of investigation is its two-pronged aspect. The investigation will necessarily be conducted with an administrative along with a criminal focus. The former is procedural and is the investigation into whether proper policy was followed and not violated. The latter involves a criminal review, and whether criminal proceedings will follow. Because these incidents are so significant, it is imperative that the investigation be complete (Cunningham, 2021).

False Statements/Perjury

These allegations are of particular importance since they speak to the integrity of the officer and the profession. Although they are far less common than other allegations, they are particularly egregious. They are handled as all allegations should be—professionally, dispassionately, and completely.

Once again, begin the case documentation with a review and discussion of the complaint. Is this court originated, or from an administrative hearing? Make sure to review all the documents that were provided in the initial complaint. Is the allegation clearly identified? Or is other official paperwork needed? Make sure to confer with the prosecuting attorney if the matter is criminal. Their guidance will determine how the investigator proceeds with interviews, evidence, etc., especially if the incident is part of a sealed court record.

Conduct background checks on the subject officer and any other individuals involved. Obtain and review any arrest reports, along with supporting documents, relevant testimony, and court records. Incorporate the summaries of these reviews into the investigative folder.

The intent here is to find the exact wording that is being considered perjury. What is the rationale behind the allegation? What is the supporting evidence? Was the officer confronted about the false statement? Was the officer provided an opportunity to clarify previous statements? It will be the investigator's task to document this information, with the direction and guidance of a prosecuting attorney if the offense is criminal.

False statements provided in an administrative hearing are somewhat easier to handle and follow similar investigative steps. Typically, officers are warned about the consequences of providing false information at the start of the official interview.

Should the officer be caught in a false statement, the investigator should provide them with the opportunity to clarify or modify their statement. Faulty recollections happen, and the officer should be allowed to correct a mistake. It is sound investigative policy that the investigator already knows all of the facts and can use that to confront the officer about their statements (Boyle & Vullierme, 2018).

Should the officer insist on letting their statement stand, without changes, the investigator documents it and confers with those agency members involved in administrative discipline. Be guided by their instructions and provide any documents they may require for disciplinary procedures.

Quota Allegation

Typically, these allegations almost always come from other police personnel, but can originate from the community. In any case, the investigation requires at least three specific investigative steps (NJOAG, 2017).

The first requirement is that there is an identified complainant. This means the complaint cannot be anonymous since the investigator may need this individual to testify in the future in an administrative hearing or criminal trial. Investigate anonymous complaints because it is part of the internal affairs investigative duty, and the investigation should be thorough. This needs to be a comprehensive record of the incident complained of and will inform future investigations.

Second, determine a specific violation of the law. What criminal actions support the allegation?

Third, locate any corroborating evidence. What evidence supports the allegation? This is problematic because officers are required to engage in law enforcement as part of their duties. In particularly criminogenic neighborhoods, much arrest activity does not necessarily indicate a quota requirement. It was the author's personal experience that these were challenging investigations because of officer reluctance to offer information and the public's propensity to provide incorrect information. Your challenge will be to determine summary activity during the normal course of policing and distinguish that from a requirement to meet a certain enforcement expectations.

A typical investigation into this allegation begins with a comprehensive review of the initial complaint recorded during intake. Determine exactly what was complained of. This will guide the rest of the investigation (NJOAG, 2017).

Obtain any pertinent records that can corroborate or refute the allegation. Review records that may be relevant to the allegation. Arrests, summonses, days off, are all important to determine if there is a pattern. Is the activity reflective of what other officers working in a similar enforcement capacity?

Find out what is going on in the workplace where the allegation is alleged to be occurring. Attempt to identify the workplace culture and the work dynamics that are ongoing. If the investigator has undercover operatives within the division that work at the location, attempt to gather information from them. Be specific about what the investigator is looking for. Information from these resources may uncover information not considered before. These assets already have an established history in the work location and can be an invaluable source of information.

Conduct background checks on the police officers assigned to the specific shift complained of, not just the subject. The investigator may be able see a pattern, or not, of quota abuse. This review may be far-reaching and time-consuming but may establish differences in activity between sections. If this is uncovered, determine why this occurring. It may not be a quota requirement.

Finally, conduct the administrative interviews. These interviews will be necessary for the police officers and their supervisors. All will be able to provide information that provides a well-rounded perspective of what is going on.

Processing an Arrested Officer

When the internal investigation results in an arrest of the officer, the investigator will be required to follow the criminal jurisdiction's policies and guidelines for arrests. Typical steps to initiate a prosecution include a police complaint, district attorney conferral, and the accusatory instrument. There is no way to circumvent the process, but there are steps the investigator can take to facilitate the process (NJOAG, 2017).

The first and foremost consideration is that the arrested employee is a member of the investigator's agency. Sworn employees have undergone the same application process as the investigator and the investigator should be mindful of that. Accordingly, this employee should be afforded the same courtesies that are afforded to all employees. It will go a long way towards a smooth processing process, no matter how distasteful. It also reduces the potential for allegations and lawsuits.

Along with this requirement for professionalism, the investigator needs to make sure that the arrested employee has minimal contact with non-police personnel currently being processed through the system. An arrested police employee, due to their affiliation with a law enforcement agency may be assaulted if kept in a holding area with other arrestees. No matter the personal feelings, the investigator has a duty to protect them from violence. Thankfully, this can be done through a simple notification during the arrest processing process. It has been the author's personal experience that this facilitates a smooth, painless arrest processing.

As soon as the investigator knows that a police employee will be arrested, they need to notify the prosecuting attorney and the arrest intake location. This allows all involved to coordinate a pause in general operations and facilitate the intake and processing of the arrested employee by themselves. This is important for the employee's safety during arraignment. If the arrested employee will be incarcerated pending further adjudication, the notification informs the jail that a high risk, sensitive person is entering the system. While never a guarantee of complete safety, the notification goes a long way to ensuring a safe arrest processing. Corrections officials can implement their protective policies for sensitive prisoners at this time, without gaps in custodial services.

In addition, the notification benefits the investigator. When following the prisoner intake procedure, the notification will allow Intake the time to be properly prepared before the arrested employee arrives. A forced pause in operations will allow the investigator and the prisoner to move through the system quickly and efficiently. The various intake steps can be completed without interference, hindrance, and long waits. Be aware, this notification may facilitate another way to process the employee (NYPD, 2016).

It is possible, if allowed, to process the employee in a private room without having to go through the general prisoner intake process. In this model, an investigator goes through the intake process without the employee. The investigator may have to take a photograph and take prints at a specific station, and this should be done with as much privacy as possible without other arrestees nearby. Other than that, the employee can wait in a separate office without subjecting them to the potential hazards of a holding cell. The arrestee will be required to be under uninterrupted observation, which necessitates an additional internal investigator, preferably someone of superior rank. Streamlining the intake process with these steps can simplify the process and will benefit the investigator, the system, and the employee.

Changing an Officer's Duty Status

Depending on the type of duty status change, certain police items will have to be obtained and secured. This duty status change could be a full suspension, where the officer has no enforcement rights, or a modification of their duty status, where they are relegated to administrative duties only, with no enforcement authority. Regardless of the status change, removing firearms is the biggest priority. This removal should consist of duty weapons, and any additional privately owned firearms. There will be challenges with securing these privately owned firearms since most rifles and shotguns are not registered. The investigator will need to make sure that the officer surrenders them voluntarily, since securing them is important for everyone's safety. The officer will also need to surrender, in most instances, their department-issued identification card and shield. Depending on the status change, the investigator may also have to obtain other department-issued property (radios, cell phones, tablets, body-worn cameras, etc.). All of these items need to be documented appropriately and stored for safekeeping pending a restoration to duty or otherwise (NYPD, 2016).

Monitoring Court Proceedings

In the instance when an officer is at trial, the investigator must document court proceedings and include them in the investigative case folder. Documentation should begin with the details about the specific court, assigned judge and prosecutor and include a short pedigree of the officer. The next section should consist of a concise summary of the investigation and the circumstances surrounding the arrest of the officer. This is to allow readers to understand the context of the prosecution. The next part summarizes the court proceedings for the specific day and any future events. Were proceedings adjourned? For what reasons? Was a plea negotiated? What was it? The final part documents the next hearing date, if necessary. Make sure all of these reports are included in the investigative file.

Case Closing Reports

Investigations are closed only when specific criteria are met. This usually occurs when all relevant investigative steps have been completed and a disposition is determined. This can only happen once the investigator can definitively say that the required steps were pursued and exhausted, and there were no additional leads to follow up on. In this instance, it is appropriate to close the investigation and record a disposition.

There are instances, however, when the investigation results in an administrative hearing or criminal trial. Technically, the investigation is complete. The disposition, however, is still pending. In this instance, the investigator needs to follow any proceedings, and include a summary of these proceedings in the investigative case file, and only conclude the investigation when a final disposition has been reached. In all instances, any additional relevant documents need to be included in the case file. This becomes a permanent record and appropriate administrative records are amended (NYPD, 2016).

Whatever the type of allegation that was investigated, concluding documentation is an important part of the investigation. This report should be a stand-alone document that provides a concise summary of the investigation. Anyone should be able to read this report and have a solid understanding of the investigation and outcome. The report should be in a standardized format, consisting of specific sections. These sections should follow the investigative timeline, beginning with the complaint (NYPD, 2016).

The beginning section should consist entirely of case descriptive information. Here, the investigator would list the following: any complaint numbers, report numbers, significant dates--when the incident occurred, when the complaint was received, information on the subject, complainant, any statutes of limitations, investigator information, and overall investigative disposition.

The next section should consist of anything associated with the complaint. Here, the investigator will summarize the allegation and how it was received. Also, if an initial investigation was conducted, the investigator should list by whom, and when. In this section, add what was done during any canvasses, whether for video recordings, or witnesses, and the results. If the investigator obtained video, provide a brief review of what the recordings contained.

After the preceding two sections, the investigator should document interviews with the complainant and any witness. Here, the investigator should begin with the results of the background investigation (criminal identification number, pedigree information). Document how and when the complaint was received, what the allegations were, and the date of the incident (NYPD, 2016).

After listing the identifying information, summarize the interviews. These interviews were already summarized in the investigative case folder and should only consist of important, relative facts. Provide a relevant summary, and identify whether the interview was with a complainant, or a witness. The reader should be able to understand the main points of the interview, without having to refer to the interview report in the investigative folder. That can always be done should there be a need.

The next section is reserved for the subject of the investigation. Briefly explain how the complainant, or witness identified the subject. Remember, the investigator has already listed subject descriptive information in the first section and doesn't need to be redundant. Keeping it simple goes a long way towards investigative efficiency. It also makes the report easier to read (NYPD, 2016).

The next section consist of the records review. Any documents relevant to the investigation are included in these sections. Separate internal agency records related to the incident from the general computer and background records the investigator accessed as part of conducting the background checks.

The agency records section consists of the agency documents related to the incident. In the instances where the complaint originated because of an arrest, the investigator needs to review intake records, complaint and arrest reports, any property receipts, and anything else related to the incident. For example, orders of protection come to mind, or anything else unique to the incident. List all the documents by record or serial number, or any other identifying number unique to the incident (NYPD, 2016).

After the investigator completed the section that memorializes all relevant incident records, the investigator needs to include the results of any computer-related, or background checks that were conducted. Depending on the incident and allegation, this can be quite extensive. Here, the investigator wants to develop profiles for all the people involved in the investigation. The importance of this cannot be overstated. Document a history for everyone. Some of these checks are required of all investigations, such as individual backgrounds, and others are dictated by the incident. Make sure to provide only summaries. All of this information was already documented extensively in the investigative case folder.

The next section should document any consultations that the investigator conducted during the investigation. Were other agencies consulted? Or was the District

Attorney contacted as in the case of a criminal investigation? Document the reason for the consultation and the results (NYPD, 2016).

The next section should document any proactive investigative steps that were conducted. Were surveillances conducted of peoples, or places? Were debriefings or integrity tests conducted? Or other similar investigative steps? In this section, outline the reasons and corresponding results of the activity.

The next section is for any other investigative activity that was not already captured in a previous section or can be used to elaborate on information not explained to satisfaction in any previous sections. Much will already have been documented in previous sections, but this section can be used for anything not already mentioned, as in investigative steps unique to this investigation and not ordinarily conducted. This section is only necessary for information not already documented, or for anything that needs to be embellished.

This next section summarizes relevant subject interviews. Since this was already documented extensively in the investigative file, this section should provide details on when the interview was conducted, who was present, and a summary of the interview. Only a summary of the main points is necessary.

The final section is a summary of the investigative conclusions. In this section, summarize the allegations, the investigative steps taken and the investigative findings. Make sure to provide the factual support for these findings, whatever they are (NYPD, 2016).

After the investigative conclusions, the investigator should list relevant attachments as appendices. This section is reserved for disposition letters, where the complainant is provided the investigative disposition. Also, any subsequent administrative or criminal action related to the incident are included. The intent is to list what occurred as a result of the investigation with supporting documents included as attachments.

Once the closing report is completed, the investigator needs to review the entire investigative file to make sure all required steps were undertaken.

Ensure that the Table of Contents is accurate and complete. Make sure that all the investigative reports are listed in the proper order and all supporting documents are included as attachments and are properly documented in the investigative reports. Ensure the accuracy of all reference numbers, names, and locations. Carefully review the closing report for accuracy, grammar, and spelling. Nothing detracts from the legitimacy of a report like improper writing. If needed, ask someone for help with this review.

This closing report format is offered as a way to provide a concise summary of an investigation, as a stand-alone report of the case file. A copy is included with the investigative folder and the original is used as a historical reference for recordkeeping. When stored in different locations, it is important to identify where the investigative folder is kept and how to access it, should the need arise.

Investigative Dispositions

After the investigation is completed, the investigator needs to assign two dispositions to the investigation--a disposition to each of the allegations that were either listed in the original complaint or were uncovered during the investigation and an overall disposition. This overall disposition will be determined by the findings for the individual allegations.

Although there are many types of dispositions, the following are the used most often and will become part of the investigative process. Always attempt to conduct a complete and comprehensive investigation, leaving no room for doubt. It is an imperative that the investigation be thorough Once completed, specific dispositions should be assigned.

Substantiated means that the complaint was determined to be true; the subject committed the action. Depending on the agency's policy and the egregiousness of the allegation, some sort of punitive sanction will be warranted (NYPD, 2016).

Partially Substantiated is used when the subject committed part of the allegations (NYPD, 2016).

Unsubstantiated is used in those instances when the investigator was unable to verify the facts or there was just not enough evidence to establish proof. The investigator was unable to prove or disprove the complaint. This is a troublesome finding because much investigative effort will have been wasted. It was the author's experience that this finding was relatively common given all the challenges to uncovering the truth.

Unfounded, is used when the investigator determined the incident did not occur or the subject was not involved in the incident (NYPD, 2016).

Exonerated is reserved for when the investigator determines the incident occurred, but the subject's conduct was lawful and proper, in accord with agency policy (NYPD, 2016).

Other Misconduct Noted is used when the investigator discovered other misconduct during the investigation, which was not listed in the original complaint. In this instance, the investigator should add the allegation and disposition to the list of allegations against the subject (NYPD, 2016).

Completing Investigations.

Changes to investigations occur frequently. Whether technology or policy, agencies are always responding to public sentiment. This is a consequence of the police profession and affects investigations. An investigative file from 20 years ago will be considerably different from a file completed after 10 years of investigative experience, or even 1 year. Investigators constantly learn new things about their craft and investigative techniques are always changing. That is why identifying and addressing investigative gaps and deficiencies is so important.

The Army conducts after action reviews of their events. Here, soldiers discuss what went well, what did not go so well, and how a similar event conducted in the future can be better. In similar fashion, investigators and their supervisors should follow a similar model. Too many times in law enforcement, the deficiency becomes the paramount focus and the determination for any sanction. Although this is important, it misses the intent of the review (CAC, 2013).

The review should be part of investigator development. It is a chance to discuss what went well, what did not go so well, and how similar events in the future can be handled successfully. Any deficiencies are a direct reflection on supervision, or in this case, lack thereof. Barring any truly egregious investigative deficiency, which probably indicates that the investigator is not suitable for this type of work and may better serve the agency elsewhere, these reviews should have a positive connotation. Although this is contrary to the bureaucratic nature of police agencies, these reviews contribute greatly to achieving a constructive work environment, rather than the miserable, toxic conditions associated with conducting internal investigations.

References

Boyle, M., & Vullierme, J. C. (2018). *A brief introduction to investigative interviewing: A practitioner's guide*. Council of Europe.

Combined Arms Center-Training. (2013). *The leader's guide to after-action reviews (aar)*. Training Management Directorate.

Cuncic, A. (2022, February 18). *The psychology behind police brutality*. Verywell Mind. https://www.verywellmind.com/the-psychology-behind-police-brutality-5077410

Cunningham, M. (2021, February 21). *A guide to conducting bifurcated police use of force investigations*. ShotSpotter. https://www.shotspotter.com/blog/police-use-of-force-investigations-guide/

Gehl, R. (2017). Introduction to criminal investigation: Processes, practices and thinking. *BCcampus*.

Heffernan, W. C., & Kleinig, J. (2004). *Private and public corruption*. Rowman & Littlefield Publishers.

Kleinig, J. (2012). *The ethics of policing*. Cambridge University Press.

LeadsOnline. (2022, September 20). *LeadsOnline*. https://www.leadsonline.com/main/index.php.

New Jersey, Office of the Attorney General. (2017). *Internal affairs policy & procedures*. https://www.nj.gov/oag/dcj/agguide/internalaffairs2000v1_2.pdf

NYPD. (2016). *Internal affairs bureau procedural guide*. NYC.

Prison Legal News. (n.d.). *Cellular telephone subpoena guide*. https://www.prisonlegalnews.org/media/publications/Cellular%20Telephone%20Subpoena%20Guide.pdf

U.S. Department of Justice, Office of Community Oriented Policing Services. (2020). Domestic violence 101: How should a law enforcement agency respond. *Community Policing Dispatch, 23*(10) https://cops.usdoj.gov/html/dispatch/10-2020/domestic_violence_101.html

Uritox. (2022). *Police officers: Complete drug test guide*. https://www.drugtestpanels.com/blogs/articles/police-officers-complete-drug-test-guide-2021#:~:text=a%20drug%20test%3F-,Do%20police%20officers%20get%20drug%20tested%3F,they%20protect%20depend%20on%20it

Lessons Learned

This section is a summary of things to consider when conducting internal investigations. They come from my own 7 years of lived experience in doing this sort or work and can assist the investigator in conducting successful investigations. This list is not exhaustive. New and unexpected contingencies arise frequently; new tactics, legal decisions, and investigative techniques come to the fore unexpectedly. It is the consequence of society. In addition, personal experiences and best practices will add to the list of investigative practices. What follows has been categorized by topic.

Proper Mindset

Internal investigations are distasteful. Due to the culture of policing, these cases are relegated to the lowest levels in the hierarchy of police investigative work. Most investigators assigned to policing their colleagues don't want to conduct these investigations. They are an affront to police solidarity and fly in the face of what a real investigator does—chase and catch bad guys. Yet, they are also essential to the proper function of the police within society and go a long way towards maximizing a positive agency image, irrespective of the police misconduct or corruption. Developing and maintaining a proper mindset is of paramount importance.

It is important to approach these investigations as a professional investigator, without any preconceived notions. Allegations are not created in a vacuum. They are the consequence of some sort of police activity. Whether truthful or not, it is the investigator's fundamental responsibility to determine the truth about what occurred. The facts and evidence will determine the truthfulness of the complaint. This caveat will go a long way towards a professional investigation, which reflects positively on the agency and the investigator. This is important because of the hypersensitivity of police agencies to outside criticism. It has been my experience that agencies avoid this at all costs.

Case Investigations

Know your investigation. This does not mean that the investigator must memorize every little detail. The investigator does, however, need to know the relevant facts and be able to brief others about the investigation and answer questions at any time. This is a direct reflection of the personal investigative prowess and professionalism. Be aware of any important dates. The last thing the investigator wants to do is miss an important appointment or due date. Whether an interview, or obtaining evidence, or attending a hearing, the investigator needs to make sure that they are where they are supposed to be on the correct date. Missing something important compromises the integrity of the investigation, which could result in an erroneous finding or even administrative discipline. Based on personal experience, this must be avoided at all costs since it reflects poorly on the investigator and the investigation. The investigator does not want to be associated with a poor investigation.

Interviews

When conducting interviews, it is useful to remember British Crime Scene Manager, John Cockram's operating paradigm, "assume nothing, believe nobody, check everything" (Taylor, 2012).

Record everything. The investigator wants to have an independent record of any interviews. Whether overtly, or covertly, make sure the equipment is functioning properly. Have backup recording equipment and power sources available and ready for use. Too many times, an important interview was not captured properly. These recordings become part of the investigative file as attachments.

People tend to lie. This is especially the case when there may be consequences to their statements. Or they tell the investigator what they think the investigator wants to hear. Remember to not trust anyone's statement without independent corroboration. If this is an initial interview, the investigator can always follow up with clarifying questions. Let the person speak. People will tell the investigator lots of things. The astute investigator already knows the facts and will be sure to be an active listener. This will result in interactions that capture required information, negating the necessity for follow-up interviewing (Boyle & Vullierme, 2018).

When conducting these interviews, avoid confrontation. Putting a person ill at ease will jeopardize the conversation, making it suspect. The astute investigator knows his case and can follow-up questionable statements with clarifying questions. This is only possible if the investigator knows the facts.

Make sure to record and document everything that transpires. Depending on the situation, the investigator may have to do this surreptitiously. A small recorder in a shirt pocket or held underneath an investigative notebook will accomplish the task without being threatening. Make a a permanent record of the conversation, which the investigator will incorporate into the investigative folder. Others will be able to access these records should the need arise.

Evidence

Be sure that the investigator retrieves and officially secures and processes evidence right away. Evidence, like memories, is perishable and easily lost. Surveillance cameras and cellphone records are a useful tool to identify what occurred or corroborate other investigative actions. The problem is that not all video is recorded. There are some systems that only offer a live feed, which will be of little value to the investigator in determining a past event. In this instance, find another camera, if possible. Also, those systems that do record to a hard drive, have different timeframes for their records. Verify how long the recordings are kept as soon as possible after the allegation is received. If the investigators the timeframe for video retention, the investigator will lose the evidence. Finally, because there are so many different systems on the market, the logistics of creating a copy of the recording, or downloading the section that the investigator needs, can become problematic. Here, someone with technical expertise will make the task that much easier. But don't forget the investigator's cellphone. Making a recording of a recording still captures the record.

When it comes to cellphone records, the process of retrieving records has been greatly facilitated by the various companies. Many companies have established liaisons with law enforcement and are a great assistance in retrieving relevant records (PLN, n.d.).

Reliance on Others

Don't rely on others to complete investigative steps. This is an internal investigation and everything that occurs during the investigation is the assigned investigator's responsibility. When reaching out for others to provide their expertise, make sure to follow-up. Keep it professional, but make sure to document any progress. It is important to remember, that different states have different laws regarding the capture of telephone recordings without a warrant. There are one-party states (i.e., New York) that allow any citizen to record any conversation that she is a party to be memorialized (Matthiesen et al., 2022). Other states (i.e., Massachusetts) are two-party states where this would be illegal; all parties must be aware of and consent to the recording of telephone conversations (Matthiesen et al., 2022). This may be important in the event that a confidential informant presents the investigator with a recorded audio (or video) conversation that supports the investigation. In a one-party state, as long as the investigator hasn't solicited or directed an informant to collect this material-it would be admissible in court. If the investigator became aware of this material in a two-party state, it would not only be inadmissible- but it would also be a criminal act (Matthiesen et al., 2022).

Timelines

Make sure the various investigative steps are completed steadily, in a timely manner. Document any gaps like vacations, sick leave, where there is no investigative progress. Avoid gaps where nothing was done for a lengthy period. It is embarrassing and casts a negative reflection on the investigator's abilities. Depending on the caseload, the investigator may be able to focus exclusively on one investigation. Many of us do not have this luxury, and when juggling numerous investigations, completing an investigative step on each case, once a week, goes a long way to maintaining case integrity. Also, be aware of any statute of limitations, either administratively or criminally. Missing one of these important timelines can result in the investigator receiving a negative sanction. It is something to be avoided at all costs. Maintain a calendar of important dates helps manage these dates. In fact, make every effort to document a steady and continuous activity log for each case. Allowing a case to lie dormant until the last possible moment, while not technically improper, can taint a case by providing an opening for defense attorneys to question motivation and ability.

Dealing with Subjects

The subjects of the investigation are agency employees. If both the subject and investigator are sworn law enforcement personnel, they were vetted and hired in the same way. Keep this in mind when dealing with subjects. There is no need to be arrogant or condescending. The subject is aware of what they did or did not do. There is every possibility that the subject is experiencing a great deal of remorse and humiliation. Keeping it professional keeps subjectivity away from the casework.

Remain cognizant of the possibility of deception. Subjects are motivated to tell the investigator what they think the investigator wants to hear, as long as the subject perceives a personal benefit. This may be contrary to the truth and the investigator needs a certain prowess to extract the truth from what is being said and heard. This is where an in-depth knowledge of the investigation and the person the investigator is dealing with go a long way towards obtaining actionable information.

Conduct the investigation as a professional. Remain dispassionate, regardless of the incident and avoid inflammatory conduct around the subject. Keep opinions out of the conversation with subjects. Relegate them to the realm of case management and steering. This will go a long way towards obtaining compliance from the subject. Things will go a lot easier for the investigator, especially when the investigator must handcuff an agency employee. Helping them maintain their dignity and self-respect prevents many problems and challenges that are not necessary.

Noncompliant Complainants

Complainants change their minds. Whatever the reason for the complaint, the investigator will come across complainants that no longer wish to cooperate. The allegation was made and for whatever reason, the complainant no longer wish to cooperate with the police. If this situation occurs, there are steps that can be taken take to protect the integrity of the investigation and the investigator.

At this point, the complainant is avoiding the investigator, and may have become unresponsive to inquiries. Document all attempts at contacting the complainant. Besides in person and telephone attempts, the investigator should send a certified letter to the complainant, requesting their cooperation in the investigation. The person who the letter is addressed to must sign for it, serving as proof of delivery. Once the receipt is returned, incorporate it into the investigative file. Three or four attempts at contact should suffice to indicate an unwillingness to cooperate. Closing an investigation due to an uncooperative complainant must be carefully documented and is a decision made echelons higher than the investigator.

If the investigator find that the complainant is avoiding all attempts at contact, the least the investigator should do is have the complainant sign a complaint withdrawal form. This clearly documents the complainant's intention and will be added to the investigative file (NYPD, 2016).

Consequences of an Internal Investigation

The ultimate purpose of the investigation is to determine the truth of what occurred. The problem is that factfinding may cause collateral damage. The investigator may identify additional subjects not previously identified, the investigator may find failures to comply with policy or procedure, or the investigator may find other actions totally independent of the complaint.

Uncovering these instances is the consequence of a comprehensive investigation. Often, the subject was cleared of the allegation, but received discipline because of a failure to comply with agency policy or procedure. If the subject followed agency procedure, there wouldn't this predicament. Whatever is uncovered, make sure not to take this personally. Maintaining professionalism and being dispassionate will go a long way towards helping the investigator maintain a professional work ethic and peace of mind.

Concluding Remarks

Internal investigations have become a necessary component of policing. In this changing era of policing where community partnerships are becoming increasingly important, professionally conducted internal investigations help establish and maintain agency credibility. This also goes a long way towards building trust between the police and the community.

Because of the internal nature of these investigations, agencies are susceptible to allegations of coverups. If the investigation is handled professionally, along with any independent review by a citizen oversight committee, the agency, the investigator, and the process is protected from false claims.

The ultimate purpose of these investigations is to maintain the professional image of the agency, by identifying and correctly dealing with misconduct and corruption. Because agency personnel are held to a higher standard than the general public, agencies need this investigative arm to maintain a professional, positive image as an agency there to protect and serve the public.

Types of Cases Chart

Corruption: All crimes	Misconduct: All conduct that is more egregious than a policy violation, but does not rise to the level of a crime	Policy violations: Anything that is against the rules

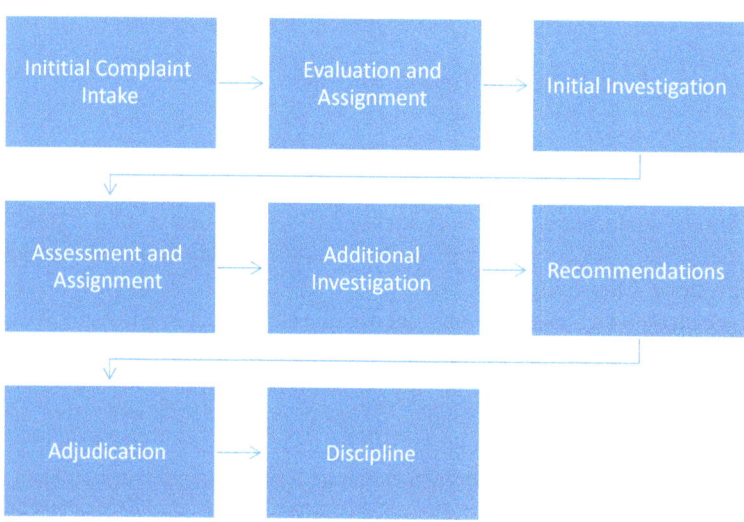

Flowchart of typical investigation

References

Boyle, M., & Vullierme, J. C. (2018). *A brief introduction to investigative interviewing: A practitioner's guide*. Council of Europe.

Matthiesen, Wickert, & Lehrer. (2022). *Laws on recording conversations in all 50 states*. https://www.mwl-law.com/wp-content/uploads/2018/02/RECORDING-CONVERSATIONS-CHART.pdf

NYPD. (2016). *Internal affairs bureau procedural guide*. NYC.

Prison Legal News. (n.d.). *Cellular telephone subpoena guide*. https://www.prisonlegalnews.org/media/publications/Cellular%20Telephone%20Subpoena%20Guide.pdf

Taylor, C. (2012, April 27). The real CSI: What happens at a crime scene. *The Guardian*. https://www.theguardian.com/science/2012/apr/27/craig-taylor-real-csi?newsfeed=true.

Additional Resources

Baker, A., & McGinty, J.C. (2010, Mar 26). NYPD confidential: NYPD police corruption and the internal affairs bureau. *NY Times.* https://www.nytimes.com/2010/03/28/nyregion/28iab.html

Brecher, J. (2014). Rotten apple corruption. In B. A. Arrigo (Ed.), *Encyclopedia of criminal justice ethics* (Vol. 1, pp. 818–820). Sage. https://doi.org/10.4135/9781452274102.n296

Cabral, S., Lazzarini, S. G., & Barbosa, A. C. Q. (2009). *Monitoring the police: An empirical study on the factors affecting the conclusion of investigation processes by an internal affairs division.* In: XIII International Society for New Institutional Economics. Hass Business School, Berkeley, CA

Davis, R., et al. (1997). *Monitoring study: A review of investigations conducted by the internal affairs bureau.* Commission to Combat Police Corruption. https://www1.nyc.gov/assets/ccpc/downloads/pdf/Monitoring-Study-A-Review-of-Investigations-Conducted-by-the-Internal-Affairs-Bureau-October-1997.pdf

DeAngelis, J., & Kupchik, A. (2007). Citizen oversight, procedural justice, and officer perceptions of the complaint investigation process. *Policing: An International Journal of Police Strategies & Management, 30*(4), 652–671.

Dijk, J. V., & Ruggiero, V. (Eds.). (2002). *Forum on crime and society* (Vol. 2, issue 1). United Nations.

Dunne, W. (2018) *The effectiveness of police 'internal affairs departments' in limiting corruption in police services – A literature review.* https://curbingcorruption.com/wp-content/uploads/2019/03/181004-Dunne-Literature-review-of-police-internal-affairs-departments.pdf

Girodo, M. (1998). Undercover probes of police corruption: Risk factors in proactive internal affairs investigations. *Behavioral Sciences and the Law, 16,* 479–496.

Griffin, C., & Ruiz, R. (1999). Sociopathic police personality: Is it a product of the "Rotten Apple" or the "Rotten Barrel?". *Journal of Police and Criminal Psychology, 14*(1), 28–37.

Gunter, W. D., & Hertig, C. A. (2005). *An introduction to theory, practice, and career development for public and private investigators.* https://www.ifpo.org/wp-content/uploads/2013/08/intro.pdf

Holmes, L. (2020, August 27). Police corruption. In *Oxford research encyclopedia of criminology.*https://oxfordre.com/criminology/view/10.1093/acrefore/9780190264079.001.0001/acrefore-9780190264079-e-633

International Association of Chiefs of Police. (2008). *Police chiefs desk reference: A strategy guide for newly appointed police leaders* (2 edition). Alexandria, VA.

Ivković, S. K. (2003). To serve and collect: Measuring police corruption. *The Journal of Criminal Law and Criminology, 93*(2/3), 593–650.

Lamboo, T. (2010). Police misconduct: Accountability of internal investigations. *International Journal of Public Sector Management, 23*(7), 613–631. https://doi.org/10.1108/09513551011078888

Maslov, A. (2015). *Measuring the performance of the police: The perspective of the public*. Public Safety Canada. https://www.publicsafety.gc.ca/cnt/rsrcs/pblctns/2015-r034/2015-r034-en.pdf

Matthiesen, W., & Lehrer. (2022). *Laws on recording conversations in all 50 states*. https://www.mwl-law.com/wp-content/uploads/2018/02/RECORDING-CONVERSATIONS-CHART.pdf

Mulcahy, A. (1995). Headhunter or real cop: Identity in the world of internal affairs officers. *Journal of Contemporary Ethnography, 24*, 99–130.

NYPD. (2006). *Searching for a known perp*. NYC.

Punch, M. (2009). *Police corruption: Deviance, accountability and reform in policing*. Willan Publishing.

Shane, J. M. (2010). Organizational stressors and police performance. *Journal of Criminal Justice, 38*, 807–818.

Sykes, G. M., & Matza, D. (1957). Techniques of neutralization: A theory of delinquency. *American Sociological Review, 22*(6), 664–670. https://doi.org/10.2307/2089195

Taylor, C. (2012, April 27). The real CSI: What happens at a crime scene. *The Guardian*. https://www.theguardian.com/science/2012/apr/27/craig-taylor-real-csi?newsfeed=true

ToersBijns, C. (2015). The Garrity rule: Know & understand the investigator's rights. *Corrections.com*. http://www.corrections.com/news/article/39796-the-garrity-rule-know-understand-the-investigatorr-rights

Twersky-Glasner, A. (2005). Police personality: What is it and why are they like that? *Journal of Police and Criminal Psychology, 20*, 56–67. https://doi.org/10.1007/BF02806707

U.S Department of Justice Archives. (2022). *Restrictions on the possession of firearms by individuals convicted of a misdemeanor crime of domestic violence*. https://www.justice.gov/archives/jm/criminal-resource-manual-1117-restrictions-possession-firearms-individuals-convicted

U.S. Department of Justice, Office of Community Oriented Policing Services. (2007). *Building trust between the police and the citizens they serve: An internal affairs promising practices guide for local law enforcement*. https://cops.usdoj.gov/RIC/Publications/cops-w0724-pub.pdf

U.S. Department of Justice, Office of Justice Programs. (1989). *Perfect partners: Co-production and crime prevention*. https://www.ojp.gov/pdffiles1/Digitization/140663NCJRS.pdf

Verry, R. A. (2011). *Mechanics of a police internal affairs investigation*. Looseleaf Law.

Warnken, B. L. (1987). The law enforcement officers' privilege against compelled self-incrimination. *University of Baltimore Law Review, 16*(3), 452–537.

Williams, A. (2019). *Understanding effects of corruption on law enforcement and environmental crime*. Bergen: U4 Anti-Corruption Resource Centre, Chr. Michelsen Institute. https://www.u4.no/publications/understanding-effects-of-corruption-on-law-enforcement-and-environmental-crime

Index

A
Administrative, 4, 21–24, 27, 33, 34, 37, 41–44, 47–52, 54, 58
Allegations, 3–5, 7, 11, 14, 15, 17, 18, 21–27, 29, 33–43, 46, 48–50, 52–55, 57, 59, 61, 62
Arrests, 21, 23, 26, 29, 36, 39, 40, 48–50, 52, 53
Association with criminals, 38–39

C
Case assessment, 24
Case assessment and classification, 24
Case closing reports, 52–54
Case investigations, 14, 58
Challenges, 8, 12–13, 49, 51, 55, 61
Changing an officer's duty status, 51
Classification, 21–30
Completing investigations, 55–56
Consequences of internal investigations, 61
Corruption, 3, 7, 12, 18–19, 21, 29, 35, 38, 42, 46, 57, 62
Criminal, 5, 11–13, 19, 21–24, 26, 27, 30, 33, 34, 38, 41, 44, 48–50, 52–54, 60

D
Dealing with subjects, 60–61
District attorney, 4, 5, 12, 21, 24, 28, 33, 38, 39, 43, 44, 47, 50, 54
Domestic incidents, 44–46
Drug screening, 41–43
Drug use, 22, 39, 41–42

E
Environmental theory, 19
Evidence, 7, 15, 23–25, 36, 39, 41, 42, 44, 46–49, 55, 57–59

F
False statements/perjury, 39, 48–49
Force incidents, 46–48

G
Garrity rule, 34

I
Initial investigation, 23–25, 36, 53
Intake, 8, 23–26, 36, 49–51, 53
Integrity test, 26, 29–30, 38, 42, 54
Internal affairs, 12, 13, 17, 18, 43, 49
Interviews, 8, 13, 25, 27, 28, 33, 34, 36, 39, 43–48, 50, 53, 54, 58–59
Investigations, 1, 3–8, 11–15, 17, 18, 21–29, 33–50, 52–62
Investigative dispositions, 52, 54, 55
Investigative flowchart, 62
Investigative steps, 4, 5, 8, 14, 21, 23, 25–29, 34–37, 40, 41, 44, 48, 49, 52, 54, 59, 60

L
Lessons learned, 57–62

M

Mindset, 5, 8
Misconduct, 3, 5, 7, 12, 13, 17–19, 21, 22, 24–26, 30, 35, 38, 42, 46, 55, 57, 62
Monitoring court proceedings, 52

N

Narcotics, 39–41
Neutralization theory, 18, 19
Noncompliant subject, 61

O

Officer-involved DWI arrests, 43–44
Oversight, 5–7, 13, 27, 62

P

Perspective, 1, 4, 8, 12, 17–19, 27, 43, 45, 50
Planting/padding (flaking), 39
Police, 1, 3–8, 12, 13, 17–19, 21–23, 25–27, 29, 35–57, 61, 62
Politics, 7–8

Proactive measure, 29
Processing an arrested officer, 50–51
Proper mindset, 17, 57

Q

Quota, 49–50

R

Reliance on others, 59–60
Rotten apple theory, 19

S

Subculture, 5, 17–19
Supervisor, 7, 8, 11–15, 17, 23, 25, 27, 30, 34, 43, 50, 56

T

Theories of misconduct/corruption, 18, 19
Timelines, 14, 22, 25, 42, 52, 60
Types of cases, 62–63

GPSR Compliance

The European Union's (EU) General Product Safety Regulation (GPSR) is a set of rules that requires consumer products to be safe and our obligations to ensure this.

If you have any concerns about our products, you can contact us on

ProductSafety@springernature.com

In case Publisher is established outside the EU, the EU authorized representative is:

Springer Nature Customer Service Center GmbH
Europaplatz 3
69115 Heidelberg, Germany